Python GUI Programming with PyQt

A Beginner's Guide to Python 3 and GUI Application Development

Legal & Disclaimer

The information contained in this book and its contents is not designed to replace or take the place of any form of medical or professional advice; and is not meant to replace the need for independent medical, financial, legal or other professional advice or services, as may be required. The content and information in this book has been provided for educational and entertainment purposes only.

The content and information contained in this book has been compiled from sources deemed reliable, and it is accurate to the best of the Author's knowledge, information, and belief. However, the Author cannot guarantee its accuracy and validity and cannot be held liable for any errors and/or omissions. Further, changes are periodically made to this book as and when needed. Where appropriate and/or necessary, you must consult a professional (including but not limited to your doctor, attorney, financial advisor or such other professional advisor) before using any of the suggested remedies, techniques, or information in this book.

Upon using the contents and information contained in this book, you agree to hold harmless the Author from and against any damages, costs, and expenses, including any legal fees potentially resulting from the application of any of the information provided by this book. This disclaimer applies to any loss, damages or injury caused by the use and application, whether directly or indirectly, of any advice or information presented, whether for breach of contract, tort, negligence, personal injury, criminal intent, or under any other cause of action.

You agree to accept all risks of using the information presented in this book.

You agree that by continuing to read this book, where appropriate and/or necessary, you shall consult a professional (including but not limited to your doctor, attorney, or financial advisor or such other advisor as needed) before using any of the suggested remedies, techniques, or information in this book.

Table of Contents

1. Introduction

Python is a general purpose scripting language which supports multiple programming paradigms such as procedural programming, object oriented programming and functional programming. Python was conceived in 1980s when a Dutch programmer named ***Guido van Rossum*** started working on the successor of ***ABC Programming language*** at ***Centrum Wiskunde & Informatica, Amsterdam***. The first version of Python then appeared in the 1990s.

Python is a cross platform interpreted language. A Python interpreter sits on the host systems which executes a Python script line by line. This is a different approach as compared to programming languages such as C, C++, Java, etc. where a compiler is used to compile the entire code into executable code (bytecode in case of Java) which is native to the host platform. Being a cross platform language, a Python script once written will execute anywhere regardless of the hardware/software platform as long as a Python interpreter is present on that system. For example, if you write a Python script on a Windows machine, you can take that script to MAC, Linux, FreeBSD machines (having Python interpreter) and it should run without any problems. One exception to this is – there should not be platform specific code in your script.

One of the core philosophy of Python is code readability. Many of the statements are meaningful in nature and more English-like as compared to other programming languages.

There are many implementations of Python. The most widely used one is ***CPython*** which is a reference implementation and serves as a base for many other implementations. ***CPython*** is written in ***C*** and ***Python***. Other well-known implementations are – ***IronPython*** (Written in C# For .NET framework, runs within .NET's common language runtime) and ***Jython*** (Written in Java, runs within Java Virtual Machine).

What is the number 3 in Python 3?

The number 3 in Python 3 states the version. Python has two major versions – ***Python 2*** and ***Python 3***. While both versions are used today, Python 2 is used for legacy software while Python 3 is futuristic. Considering the future value, we will be learning Python 3 in this book.

What are the Prerequisites for learning Python?

In my opinion, no previous programming background is needed to learn Python. Will definitely help if you do have any programming knowledge. However, you should be comfortable with using the ***Command Prompt*** on ***Windows*** and ***Shell/Terminal*** on ***Linux***. For GUI application development, it is advisable to have some programming background.

2. Scope

Being a general purpose, multi-paradigm cross platform scripting language, Python is in great demand today. According to ***IEEE Spectrum***, Python is the best programming language of 2019 followed by Java and C. It is possible to develop desktop applications, web applications, web services, etc. in Python. Along with that, Python can also be used in Data Science, BigData, Machine Learning, Cloud Computing, etc. In Embedded Systems and IoT also, Python remains very much relevant. Nowadays, ARM powered single board computers (SBCs) such as Raspberry Pi, Asus Tinkerboard S, BeagleBone, Banana Pi, Odroid XU4, etc. are very popular for Embedded Systems and IoT prototyping. Most of these boards can run Embedded Linux and as a result they can run Python. There is a special Python implementation called MicroPython which is meant for developing firmware for Arduino and other microcontrollers and System on Chip (SoC) such as STM-32, ESP8266, ESP32, etc.

Python applications can be extended using other languages such as C, C++, Java, etc. You can make use of libraries from other languages in Python and you can also call Python scripts/libraries from other languages. This opens up a world of possibilities of what one can do with Python.

Python is also very well equipped to access databases such as MSSQL, Oracle, MySQL, PostgreSQL, SQLite, etc.

Some of the very well-known software and web applications/ services such as Instagram, Dropbox, YouTube, Yahoo Maps, BitTorrent, etc. are written in Python either partially or fully.

What will I learn from this book?

This book is divided into two parts – ***Python programming*** and ***GUI application development***. In the Python programming part, you will learn to write basic to intermediate Python console applications making use of the various programming constructs and included libraries. In the GUI application development part, you will learn to develop basic GUI applications using Qt/PyQt.

What is Qt and PyQt?

Qt is a cross platform GUI application development framework available for Windows, Linux, MAC and Embedded Systems. PyQt is a Qt Binding for Python. Earlier in this chapter we saw that Python can be extended using other languages, this is one small application of that. The native development language of Qt is C++. PyQt is a Qt wrapper using which Qt classes and functions can be accessed using Python instead of C++.

3. Getting Started

You will need a PC/Laptop with Windows/Linux or a MAC system to write and execute Python programs. Python programs can be written using any text editor including Notepad. I suggest ***Notepad++*** (https://notepad-plus-plus.org/). Simple Python programs are plain-text files and carry the extension ***.py***. Other extensions of Python file types are – ***.pyc, .pyd, .pyz, .pyo and .pyw***. We will only be working with the ***.py*** file type.

A Python interpreter is needed to execute python scripts. In this section we will see how to install a Python interpreter.

3.1 Installing Python on Windows

Log on to – https://www.python.org/downloads/ and download the latest version of Python 3. Once you have the installation file, execute it. You will need Administrator rights to do install Python on your system. The installation process should begin and you should see a window like this:

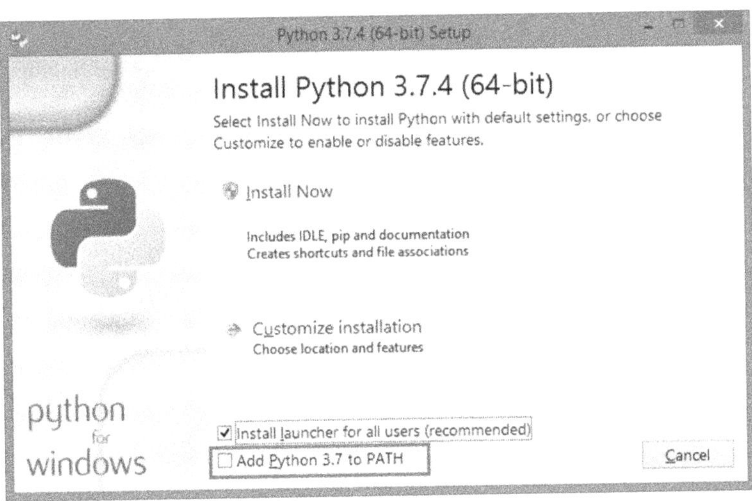

Check ***"Add Python 3.x to PATH"*** option and click ***Install Now***. It is advisable to keep other options unchanged unless you are a fairly advanced computer user and you know what you are doing.

The installation process should begin and you should be able to check out the progress with a Window that looks like this:

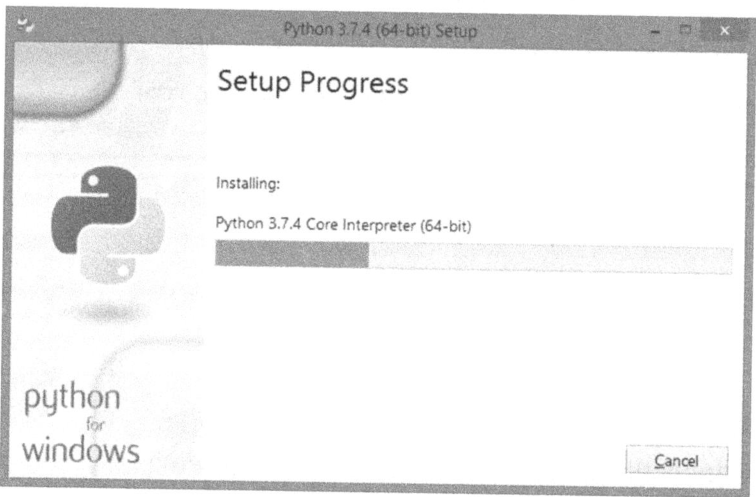

Once the installation process finishes, open ***Command Prompt***, type ***python*** and hit Enter. If you should see something like this:

```
C:\Windows\System32\cmd.exe - python
F:\>python
Python 3.7.4 (tags/v3.7.4:e09359112e, Jul  8 2019, 20:34:20) [MSC v.1916 64 bit
(AMD64)] on win32
Type "help", "copyright", "credits" or "license" for more information.
>>>
```

If you see an error message like – ***"python" is not recognized as an internal or external command, operable program or batch file***, it means either Python has not been properly installed or the ***PATH*** variable has not been properly set.

3.2 Installing Python on Linux or MAC

It is most likely that Python came bundled with your operating system if you are using Linux or macOS. It is also possible that it is Python 2 instead of Python 3. Newer MAC/Linux distributions will have Python 3. Some will have both Python 2 and Python 3. Here is how you check – open Terminal/Shell, type ***python*** and hit Enter. If you see a Python console like the one shown in the image below, it means python is present:

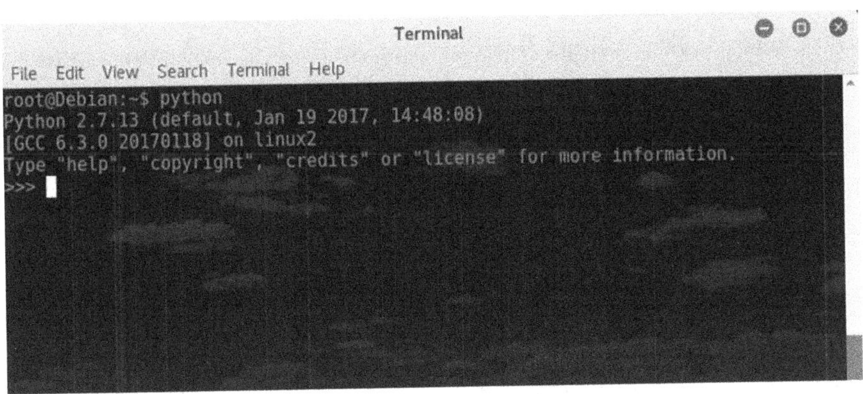

This will show you the version of python on the first line but there is a better version to determine the version. Type the following command and hit Enter:

$>python --version

Here, you will determine whether you have Python 2 or Python 3. If you have Python 2, check if you also have Python 3. To do so, type ***python3*** and hit Enter. If you see a Python 3 console like the one shown in the image below, it means Python 3 is also present:

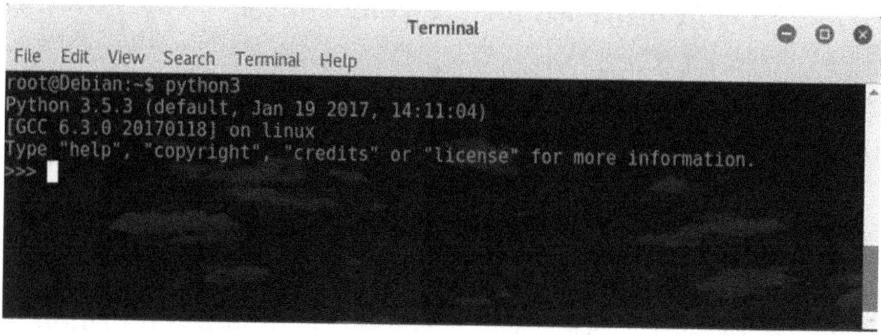

```
Terminal
File  Edit  View  Search  Terminal  Help
root@Debian:~$ python3
Python 3.5.3 (default, Jan 19 2017, 14:11:04)
[GCC 6.3.0 20170118] on linux
Type "help", "copyright", "credits" or "license" for more information.
>>>
```

You could check the exact version of Python 3 using the following command:

$>python3 --version

On my Linux system, both Python 2 and Python 3 came bundled with the OS. I use ***python*** command to access the Python 2 interpreter and ***python3*** command to access the Python 3 interpreter. This may not be the case always. You could have a newer OS where in you could access Python 3 interpreter using the ***python*** command (and not ***python3***).

If there is only Python 2 on your system, it is of no use to you in learning concepts from this book and you will have to install Python 3. Go to https://www.python.org/downloads/, download the relevant file for your OS and install Python 3. If you have both Python 2 and Python 3, you need to use Python 3.

3.3 Writing Python Scripts

As mentioned earlier, Python scripts can be written using any text editor. I personally prefer using ***Notepad++*** but you can use any other text editor such as Notepad, WordPad, gedit, KEdit, vi, emacs, etc. In short, a script is written as plaintext and saved using the extension ***.py***. This file is referred to as a python script, code, program, source code, source file or simply source.

On Unix based operating systems such as Linux, MAC and FreeBSD, the first line of the code should be a shebang line pointing to the exact location of the Python interpreter. The shebang line is a sequence of characters beginning with ***#!*** followed by the location of the interpreter. The Python interpreter is usually located at ***/usr/bin/*** or ***/usr/local/bin/*** directory on Unix based systems. If you access Python 3 interpreter using ***python*** command, your shebang line will look like this:

#!/usr/bin/python

OR

#!/usr/local/bin/python

If you access Python 3 interpreter using ***python3*** command, your shebang line will look like this:

#!/usr/bin/python3

OR

#!/usr/local/bin/python3

You can alternatively point the shebang line to the ***env*** command (usually located at ***/usr/bin/env***) and use it to invoke the Python interpreter as follows:

#!/usr/bin/env python

OR

#!/usr/bin/env python3

Without a shebang line, the script will work fine most of the time. We will learn more about what happens when you do not include a shebang line later in this chapter.

On Windows, there is no concept of a shebang line and hence you can skip it.

3.4 Executing Python scripts on Windows

A Python script can be executed using the following command in the Command Prompt:

python <script name>

If the script name is ***myscript.py***, the above command will look like:

python myscript.py

3.5 Executing Python scripts on Linux or MAC

On Unix based systems, Python scripts can be executed in two ways – by invoking the python interpreter through the shell/terminal and by making the script executable by giving it appropriate permissions.

3.5.1 Invoking Python Interpreter

Executing a script by invoking the python interpreter is straight forward. All you have to do is open the shell/terminal and execute the following command:

python <script name>

OR

python3 <script name>

If the script name is ***myscript.py***, the above command will look like:

python myscript.py

OR

python3 myscript.py

3.5.2 Making a Python script executable

A script can be made executable by giving it the execute permission using the ***chmod*** command. There are many ways in which you can use the ***chmod*** command, we will only learn the basic one. One of the simplest syntax of this command is:

chmod <permission> <files>

The permission ***+x*** is used to add execute permission and ***-x*** is used to remove execute permission. If you had a script called myscript.py and wanted to give it execute permission, you would do it as follows:

chmod +x myscript.py

More than one files can be given the same permission at once by separating the files using comma. If you had 3 scripts – ***script1.py, script2.py*** and ***script3.py*** to be made executable, you can do it in one single command as follows:

chmod +x script1.py, script2.py, script3.py

Once a script has been made executable, it can be executed as follows:

./<script name>

The ***myscript.py*** file would be executed as:

./myscript.py

For whatever reason, if you have to strip a file off its executable permission, you can use the ***-x*** flag as follows:

chmod -x myscript.py

Note: *If you want to execute a python script by making it executable, you have to include the shebang line and it should correctly point to the Python 3 interpreter. Without this, the script will not know which interpreter to invoke and the script will fail to execute.*

3.6 Script Execution Demo

Let us write and execute a python script which displays a message inside the terminal. Open your favourite text editor, copy-paste the following code and save the file as ***FirstProgram.py*** at a convenient location:

```
#First Program
print ("My first python program is working!")
```

<u>You do not have to understand how the code works for now.</u>

On ***Windows***, open ***Command Prompt***, navigate to the directory where you just saved your first python script execute the python script as follows:

python FirstProgram.py

You should see the following output:

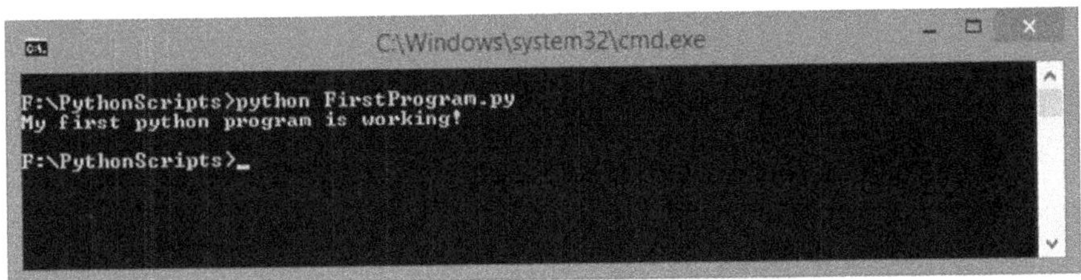

On ***Linux/MAC***, open ***Shell/Terminal***, copy paste the following code in a text editor and save it as ***FirsProgram.py***.

```
#!/usr/bin/env python3
print ("My first python program is working!")
```

You may need to edit the shebang line depending on how you invoke the Python 3 interpreter on your system.

Navigate to the directory where ***FirstProgram.py*** is present and execute the following command:

python FirstProgram.py

OR

python3 FirstProgram.py

You should see the following output:

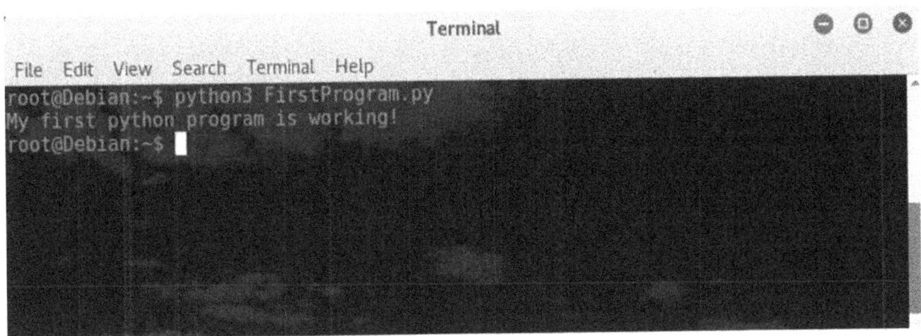

If you have figured out the correct command of Python 3 interpreter (python or python3), you can alternatively make the script executable by giving it the ***+x*** permission using ***chmod*** command and execute the script as follows:

chmod +x FirstProgram.py

./FirstProgram.py

You should see the following output:

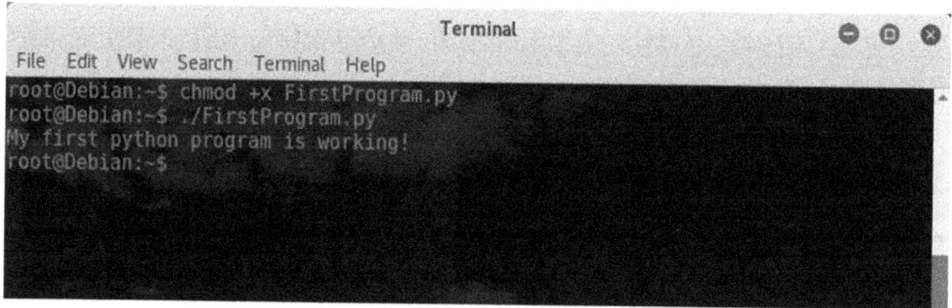

When learning Python, it does not matter whether you use Windows, Linux, FreeBSD or MAC. The scripting and execution procedure remains more or less the same. The programs demonstrated in this book are written and executed on a Windows machine. However, they should work in Linux, FreeBSD or MAC without any problems.

4. Syntax

In this section we will learn the basic syntax that needs to be followed while writing python scripts. Python is a case sensitive language. We may look at these words – "Universe" and "universe" and say that they both mean the same. But a case sensitive language will treat them differently and so does python.

4.1 Keywords

Keywords are reserved words that cannot be used as identifier names. Here is a list of Python 3 keywords that cannot be used to name variables, functions, classes, objects, etc.:

False	None	True	and	as	assert	async
await	break	class	continue	def	del	elif
else	except	finally	for	from	global	if
import	in	is	lambda	nonlocal	not	or
pass	raise	return	try	while	with	yield

4.2 Statements

A statement is used to carry out a task or a group of tasks. A script is usually made up of a group of statements that perform various tasks. A task can be anything such as performing arithmetic operations, checking if two numbers are equal, opening and reading files, etc. As we have seen earlier, Python is an interpreted language and a Python script is executed line by line. One statement is usually present on one line. Technically you can have as many statements on one line as you want by separating them using a semicolon but it is not recommended. When we say a script is executed line by line, it means that the statements are executed line by line. Here are a few examples of statements:

Country = "Singapore"

None

print ("Sample Output")

*product = 5.86 * 82.41*

flag = True

4.3 Block of Code

A block of code is a collection of several lines of statements. In Python, a block is denoted by exactly one tab-space indent. This is a very important concept. Unlike in programming languages like C, C++ or Java, there are no curly bracket to denote a block in Python. Blocks are extensively used in control structures, functions, etc. It is essential that you thoroughly understand the concept of code blocks in Python.

Consider the screenshot of the following Python script written in Notepad++:

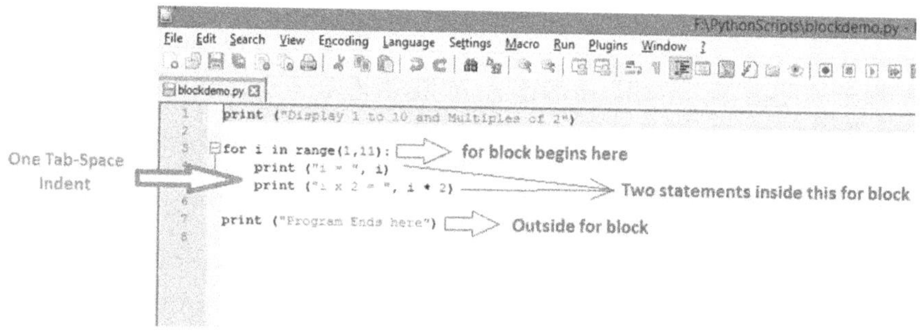

The above screenshot shows the correct way of leaving a tab-space indent in order to make use of blocks. Had there been no tab-space indent after the for statement (as shown in the image below), there would be no block.

```
print ("Display 1 to 10 and Multiples of 2")

for i in range(1,11):
print ("i = ", i)
print ("i x 2 = ", i * 2)

print ("Program Ends here")
```

No indent here, this will not work!

It is also possible to have nested code block. A nested code block is a block of code inside another block of code. The nested code block should be at another tab space indent from the previous block's indent. Consider the following screenshot of a script having nested code blocks:

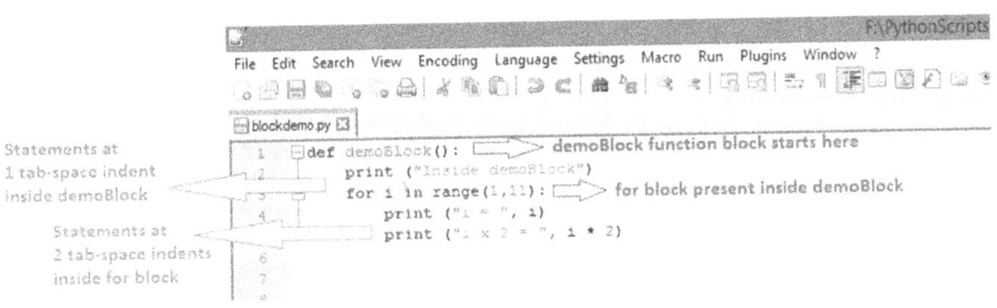

4.4 Comments

Comments are lines that are ignored by the interpreter and are used to mark, describe or explain a piece of code. There are no hard and fast rules with the usage of comments as such and since they are ignored by the interpreter, you can use them the way you see fit.

There are single line comments as well as multi-line comments.

4.4.1 Single line comments

A single line comment begins with a ***hash symbol (#)*** and ends on the same line. For example:

#This is a single line comment.
X = 8 #This is also a single line comment and will be ignored.

4.4.2 Multi-line comments

Multi-line comments are a block of comments which span over multiple lines. These have to be enclosed within ***3 single quotes (''')*** at the beginning as well as at the end. For example:

'''

Multi-line comment section has begun,
Marked by 3 single quotes. As a result, this entire
Section of comments will be ignored by the interpreter.
The following statement with 3 single quotes marks end of this comment block.
'''

Note: *This book contains many programming examples. The codes are explained in a comprehensive manner using comments. It is highly recommended that you thoroughly go through the comments in each of the included scripts.*

5. Hello World! Python Script

Python follows a top-down approach when it comes to script execution. That is, the execution will begin from the first statement and all the following statements will be executed one by one until the ***end-of-file (EOF)*** is reached or until the program is abruptly terminated internally/externally. In programming languages such as C, C++, Java and many others, there has to be a ***main*** function that serves as an entry point of the program. In python, you can optionally write a main function. Most of the programs in this book do not contain a ***main*** function.

Let us learn to write a python script to display ***Hello World!*** There is a function called ***print*** which is used to display data on the console. There are different ways of using the ***print*** function, for now, we will learn the simplest form of its usage to display a message on the console.

The syntax of ***print*** function for this case:

print (<string>)

The message we are trying to display – ***Hello World!*** is a string. A string is a sequence of characters represented in Python by enclosing them within single or double quotes (but not both in a mixed order). The string ***Hello World!*** can be represented as ***"Hello World!"*** or ***'Hello World!'*** . In order to display Hello World! using print function, the following statement can be used:

```
print ("Hello World!")
        #OR
print ('Hello World!')
```

Let us put this in a file and save it as ***HelloWorld.py***. Here is the code:

```
#This script displays Hello World! on the console
print ("Hello World!")
```

Let us execute this python script with the following command:

python HelloWorld.py

Output:

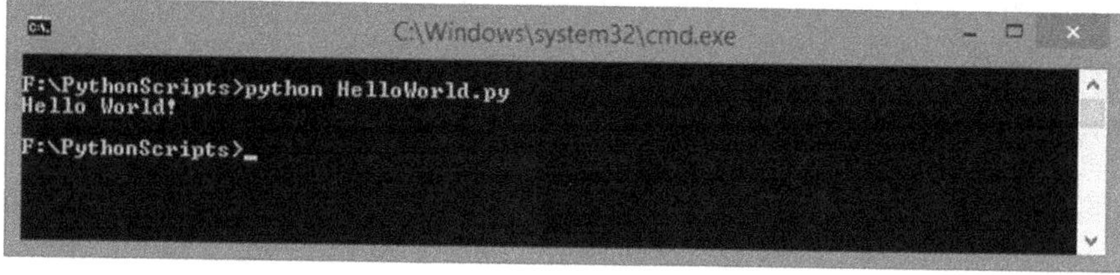

6. Variables and Data Types

One of the objectives behind learning any programming language is that we want to play with data in some way. Data can be anything from numbers, strings, to complex data types such as objects. In ***Chapter 5***, we wrote a script to display ***Hello World!*** in the console. The string that we displayed in the console was our data. Variables offer a convenient way to hold data. A variable is a name given to a memory location. When a variable is declared, according to the type of data it stores, some space is reserved for it in the system memory. This memory location can be uniquely identified using a memory address which is usually represented in Hexadecimal. It would not be possible to work with memory addresses directly every time we want to access data; Hence, we have the concept of variables.

Python can handle different kinds of data; each kind is known as a ***Data Type***. We will look at the important Data Types later in this section.

6.1 Variables

A variable name can contain letters, numbers and underscore character(s). The first character of a variable name cannot be a number. In addition to this, keywords cannot be used as variable names. To assign values to variables, we use the de-facto assignment operator given by the ***equal-to sign (=)***. The general syntax of assigning values to variables is:

<variable name> = <value>

Example:

name = "Vanessa"

num = 642

val = 4.678

The value on the right hand side of the equal-to sign is assigned to the variable on the left hand side. Explicit declaration of variables is not required. Declaration and assignment happens in one statement.

Multiple assignment of variables can be done as follows:

<variable 1> = <variable 2> = … <variable n> = <value>

Example:

a = b = c = d = 100

Here, ***a, b, c and d*** will be assigned a numeric value of ***100.***

Another way of doing a multiple assignment is:

<variable 1>, <variable 2>, … <variable n> = <value 1>, <value 2>, … <value n>

Example:

name, age, country = "Fiona", 27, "Colombia"

The above statement is equivalent to:

name = "Fiona"

age = 27

country = "Colombia"

6.2 Data Types

Python has 5 standard data types:

- Numbers
- Strings
- List
- Tuple
- Dictionary

In order to get started and be able to write beginners' scripts, you only need to understand ***Numbers*** and ***Strings***. There is a dedicated chapter on List, Tuple and Dictionary later in this book.

6.2.1 Numbers

Python supports the following types of ***Numbers***:

- int
  - Signed integers. Can also be represented in HEX format. Example:
    - *2, -6, 4, 125, 0x65*
- float
  - Floating point values. Example:
    - *4.8, -3.65, 3.0, -77.6, 25.5*
- complex
  - Complex numbers. Can have real and imaginary parts. Example:
    - *3+2j, -5.6+3j, 2.75j, -86j, 5-3j, 23j*

When working with numbers, its subtype need not be specified. A value can be directly assigned to a variable and its type will be determined implicitly.

6.2.2 Strings

There is a dedicated chapter on strings later in this book. In this section, we will learn the basics of strings just enough to get started.

A string is a sequence of characters. A variable can be assigned a string value by enclosing the sequence of characters within either double quotes or single quote. Here are a few examples:

name = "Jonathan"
address = 'Manhattan Island'
education, university = "Post-Graduate", 'UCLA'

6.3 Displaying Variable Contents

The simplest way to display variables is using the ***print*** function. General Syntax:

print (<variable>)
Example:
num = 1654
item = "HTC U12+"
print (num)
print (item)

Multiple variables can be displayed using a single ***print*** statement by separating the variables using comma as follows:

print (<variable 1>, <variable 2>, … <variable n>)

Example:

pc = "Dell Laptop"

cost = 789.00

print (pc, cost)

Constant strings and variables can be combined in a single ***print*** statement by separating constant string and/or variables using commas. Consider the following example:

name = "Shelby"

age = 31

print ("Name: ", name , "Age: ", age)

If you want to display something on a new line, you can include the escape character sequence ***"\n"*** inside the print statement.

Here is a simple python script that demonstrates the usage of variables:

```
#Variables Demo
#Initialize different variables
a = 4
b = 6.465
c = 3+2j
name, age, occupation = "Benjamin", 32, "Business
Consultant"
country = "Canada"
#Display everything
print ("a = ", a)
print ("b = ", b)
print ("c = ", c)
print ("\n\nName: ", name,
        "\nAge: ", age,
        "\nOccupation: ", occupation,
        "\nCountry: ", country, "\n")
```

Output:

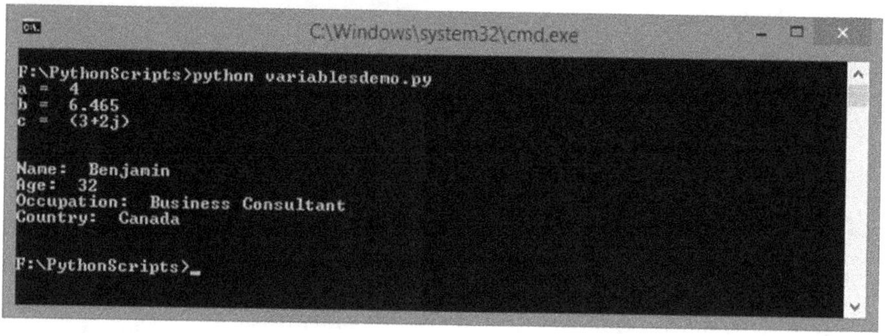

```
C:\Windows\system32\cmd.exe

F:\PythonScripts>python variablesdemo.py
a =  4
b =  6.465
c =  (3+2j)


Name:  Benjamin
Age:  32
Occupation:  Business Consultant
Country:  Canada


F:\PythonScripts>_
```

7. Operators

An operator is a symbol or a group of symbols that performs a computational task such as arithmetic operations, logical operations, binary operations, etc. Python offers ***arithmetic operators, comparison operators, logical operators, assignments operators, bitwise operators, membership operators and identity operators.*** We will cover each one of these categories except membership operators because, in order to understand this category of operators, you should understand ***Strings, Lists, Tuples or Dictionaries.*** The usage of membership operators is discussed in the relevant chapters ahead.

7.1 Arithmetic Operators

Arithmetic operators are used to perform arithmetic operations such as addition, subtraction, multiplication, division, etc.

Operator	Description	Sample Usage	Explanation
+	Addition	x + y	Computes the arithmetic sum of the given operands.
-	Subtraction	x - y	Computes the arithmetic difference of the given operands.
*	Multiplication	x * y	Multiplies operands and returns the product.
/	Division	x / y	Performs division and returns the quotient.
%	Modulus	x % y	Performs division and returns the remainder.
//	Floor Division	x // y	Performs division first and returns the floor value of the quotient. The floor function in mathematics gives the closest integer which is less than the given value. For example, floor(2.45) = 2 and floor(-4.67) = -5.
**	Exponent	x ** y	Raises the power of the operand on the left by a value of the operand on the right. For example, 2 ** 3 will return 8.

Let us write a simple python script that demonstrate the usage of arithmetic operators on two operands. The operands are assigned arbitrary values.

```
#Arithmetic operators demo
#Declare two variables, assign arbitrary values
x = 53
y = 24
#Perform Arithmetic operations, assign result to
variables
#Calculate sum
sum = x + y
#Calculate difference
difference = x - y
#Calculate product
product = x * y
#Perform division
quotient = x / y
#Modulus
mod = x % y
#Perform floor division
floor_quotient = x // y
#Exponent
exp = x ^ y
#Display everything
print("\nx = ", x , "y = ", y,
   "\nsum = ", sum ,
   "\ndifference = ", difference ,
   "\nproduct = ", product ,
   "\nquotient = ", quotient ,
   "\nremainder = ", mod ,
   "\nquotient (floor value) = ", floor_quotient ,
   "\nexponent = ", exp
   )
```

<u>Output:</u>

```
C:\Windows\system32\cmd.exe

F:\PythonScripts>python arithmeticoperators.py

x =  53 y =  24
sum =  77
difference =  29
product =  1272
quotient =  2.2083333333333335
remainder =  5
quotient (floor value) =  2
exponent =  45

F:\PythonScripts>_
```

7.2 Comparison Operators

Comparison operators, also known as relational operators are used to compare operands. These operators can check if an operand is equal to another operand, greater than another operand, etc. Depending on the outcome of the comparison, these operators return either a Boolean ***True*** or a Boolean ***False***. Comparison operators are used heavily in control structures.

Operator	Description	Sample Usage	Explanation
==	Equal To	x == y	Returns **True** if the values of the operands are equal, returns **False** otherwise.
!=	Not Equal To	x != y	Returns **True** if the values of the operands are not equal, returns **False** otherwise.
<	Less Than	x < y	Returns **True** if the value of the operand on the left is less than the value of the operand on the right, returns **False** otherwise.
>	Greater Than	x > y	Returns **True** if the value of the left operand is greater than the value of the operand on the right, returns **False** otherwise.
<=	Less Than OR Equal To	x <= y	Returns **True** if the value of the left operand is less than ***OR equal to*** the value of the operand on the right, returns **False** otherwise.
>=	Greater Than OR Equal To	x >= y	Returns **True** if the value of the left operand is greater than ***OR equal to*** the value of the operand on the right, returns **False** otherwise.

Here is a python script which performs comparison operations on two operands having arbitrary values and displays the result directly using the ***print*** function:

```
#Comparison Operators Demo
#Declare two variables
a = 126
b = 62
#Perform Relational Operations
print("\na = ", a , "b = ", b,
    "\na == b : ", a == b ,
    "\na != b : ", a != b ,
    "\na < b : ", a < b ,
    "\na > b : ", a > b ,
    "\na <= b : ", a <= b ,
    "\na >= b : ", a >= b
    )
```

Output:

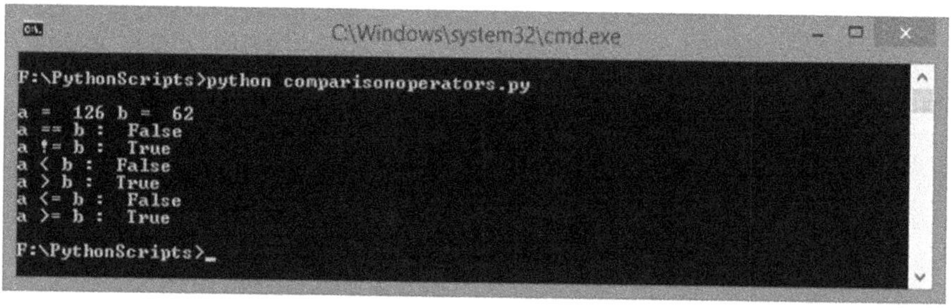

```
C:\Windows\system32\cmd.exe
F:\PythonScripts>python comparisonoperators.py

a =  126 b =  62
a == b :  False
a != b :  True
a < b :  False
a > b :  True
a <= b :  False
a >= b :  True

F:\PythonScripts>_
```

7.3 Logical Operators

Logical operators are used to perform logical operations on the given operands. Operands here have to be Boolean True or False and the outcome of such operations is Boolean True or False. Usually, these operators are used together with comparison operators.

Operator	Description	Sample Usage	Explanation
or	Logical OR	(x or y)	Compares operands and returns ***True*** if any one of the values is True, returns ***False*** otherwise .
and	Logical AND	(x and y)	Compares operands and returns ***True*** if all the values are True, returns ***False*** otherwise.
not	Logical NOT	not x	Inverts the Boolean value – not True will return ***False*** and not False will return ***True***.

Let us write a script to demonstrate the usage of logical operators alone and also comparison and logical operators together:

```
#Logical Operators Demo
#Assign Boolean Values to variables
x = True
y = False
#Display x, y and results of Logical Operations
print ("\nx = ", x, " y = ", y,
    "\nx or y = ", (x or y),
    "\nx and y = ", (x and y),
    "\nnot x = ", (not x), "\nnot y = ", (not y))
#Assign numeric values to variables
a = 45.75
b = 12
c = 32
#Use Comaprison operators alongside Logical operators
print ("\n(a > b) or (b < c) = ", (a > b) or (b <
c),
    "\n(a == b) or (b != c) = ", (a == b) or (b !=
    c),
    "\n(a < b) and (b < c) = ", (a < b) and (b < c),
    "\n(b != a) and (a != c) = ", (b != a) and (a !=
    c),
    "\n(not (a == b)) or (not (b == c)) = ", (not (a
    == b)) or (not (b == c)))
```

Output:

```
C:\Windows\system32\cmd.exe
F:\PythonScripts>python logicaloperators.py
x =  True   y =  False
x or y =  True
x and y =  False
not x =  False
not y =  True

(a > b) or (b < c) =  True
(a == b) or (b != c) =  True
(a < b) and (b < c) =  False
(b != a) and (a != c) =  True
(not (a == b)) or (not (b == c)) =  True

F:\PythonScripts>
```

7.4 Bitwise Operators

Bitwise operators work at a bit level. That is, perform operations in a bit-by-bit manner. In order to understand this class of operators, you need to understand the binary number system. In Python, you can use the function ***bin(<number>)*** to retrieve the binary equivalent of a ***<number>***. This functions will return the binary equivalent in string format. Also, you can assign to a variable the binary equivalent of a number directly by prefixing ***0b*** to the binary number. For example:

> *#The number 5 can be written as 101 in binary.*
>
> *#We can assign it to a variable as follows:*
>
> *num = 0b101*

Here is the table of Bitwise operators:

Operator	Description	Sample Usage	Explanation
|	Bitwise OR	x | y	Performs Logical OR on each of the bits of the operands.
&	Bitwise AND	x & y	Performs Logical AND on each of the bits of the operands.
^	Bitwise XOR	x ^ y	Performs Logical XOR on each of the bits of the operands.
~	Binary 1's Complement	~x	Calculate Binary 1's complement of the given operand.
<<	Left Shift	x << y	Shift left, the bits of the operand on the left by a number of times denoted by the value of the operand on the right. For example, ***x* <<*y*** means left shift the bits of ***x***, ***y*** number of times.
>>	Right Shift	x >> y	Shift right, the bits of the operand on the left by a number of times denoted by the value of the operand on the right. For example, ***x* >>*y*** means right shift the bits of ***x***, ***y*** number of times.

Following is a python script that shows the working of Bitwise operators:

```
#Bitwise Operators Demo
#Assign values to variables
x = 23
y = 29
#Display bitwise operation results
print ("\nx = ", x, " x (binary) = ", bin(x),
   "\ny = ", y, " y (binary) = ", bin(y),
   "\n~x = ", ~x, " ~x (binary) = ", bin(~x),
   "\n~y = ", ~y, " ~y (binary) = ", bin(~y),
   "\nx | y = ", x | y, " x | y (binary) = ", bin(x
   | y),
```

```
"\nx & y = ", x & y, " x & y (binary) = ", bin(x
& y),
"\nx ^ y = ", x ^ y, " x ^ y (binary) = ", bin(x
^ y),
"\nx >> 2 = ", x >> 2, " x >> 2 (binary) = ",
bin(x >> 2),
"\ny >> 4 = ", y >> 4, " y >> 4 (binary) = ",
bin(y >> 4),
"\nx << 3 = ", x << 3, " x << 3 (binary) = ",
bin(x << 3),
"\ny << 1 = ", y << 1, " y << 1 (binary) = ",
bin(y << 1)
)
```

Output:

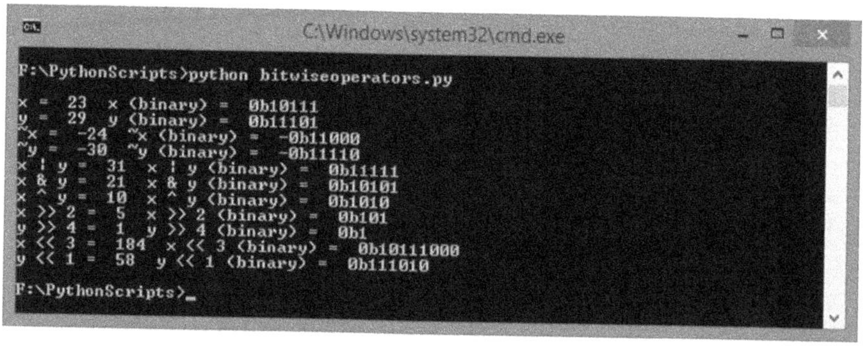

```
C:\Windows\system32\cmd.exe
F:\PythonScripts>python bitwiseoperators.py
x =  23  x (binary) =  0b10111
y =  29  y (binary) =  0b11101
~x =  -24  ~x (binary) =  -0b11000
~y =  -30  ~y (binary) =  -0b11110
x | y =  31  x | y (binary) =  0b11111
x & y =  21  x & y (binary) =  0b10101
x ^ y =  10  x ^ y (binary) =  0b1010
x >> 2 =  5  x >> 2 (binary) =  0b101
y >> 4 =  1  y >> 4 (binary) =  0b1
x << 3 =  184  x << 3 (binary) =  0b10111000
y << 1 =  58  y << 1 (binary) =  0b111010

F:\PythonScripts>_
```

7.5 Assignment Operators

We have seen the default ***assignment operator (=)*** which assigns the value on the right to the operand on the left. There are more such operators which perform an arithmetic operation first and then assign. Such operators are also known as ***compound assignment operators.***

Operator	Description	Sample Usage	Explanation
=	Assignment Operator	x = y y = a + b * c name = "Gems"	Assigns to the operand on the left the value given by the operand on the right. The left operand has to be a variable, the right operand can be a constant value, variable or an expression.
+=	Add and Assign	x += y	Computes the arithmetic sum of the given operands and assigns the resulting value to the operand on the left. ***x +=y*** is the same as ***x = x + y***.
-=	Subtract and Assign	x -= y	Computes the arithmetic difference of the given operands and assigns the resulting value to the operand on the left. ***x -=y*** is the same *as* ***x = x - y***.
*=	Multiply and Assign	x *= y	Multiplies the given operands and assigns the product to the operand on the left. ***x *= y*** is the same as ***x = x * y***.
/=	Divide and Assign	x /= y	Divides the given operands and assigns the quotient to the operand on the left. ***x /= y*** is the same as ***x = x / y***.
%=	Take Modulus and Assign	x %= y	Divides the given operands and assigns the remainder to the operand on the left. ***x %= y*** is the same as ***x = x % y***.
//=	Floor Divide and Assign	x //= y	Divides the given operands and assigns the floor value of the quotient to the operand on the left. ***x //= y*** is the same as ***x = x // y***.
**=	Take Exponent and Assign	x **= y	Raises the power of the operand on the left by a value of the operand on the right and assigns the resulting value to the operand on the left. ***x **= y*** is the same as ***x = x ** y***.

7.6 Identity Operators

Identity operators are usually used to determine whether a variable is of a certain type. These operators return ***True*** or ***False.*** These can also function as comparison operators but rarely used because we already have dedicated comparison operators. There is a built in function in Python called ***type(<variable>)*** that returns the data type of the given ***<variable>.*** Here are the identity operators.

Operator	Sample Usage	Description
is	x is y type(y) is int	Returns ***True*** if both operands are the same. ***False*** Otherwise.
is not	x is not y type (x) is not type (y)	Returns ***True*** if both operands are not the same. ***False*** Otherwise.

Let us write a python script to demonstrate the use of identity operators. We will use the ***type (<variable>)*** function to retrieve the type of the variables.

```
#Identity Operators Demo
#Initiate some variables
a = 3
b = -7.864
c = 15+23j
country = "Argentina"
#Identity operators like comparison operators
print ("\na is 3: ", (a is 3))
print ("\nb is 7.5: ", (b is 7.5))
print ("\na is not 5: ", (a is not 5))
#Display data type of all variables
print ("\n\ntype(a): ", type (a),
   "\n\ntype(b): ", type (b),
   "\n\ntype(c): ", type (c),
   "\n\ntype(country): ", type (country))
#Check whether a variable is of a certain type
print ("\n\ntype(a) is int: ", type(a) is int,
"\n\ntype(b) is int: ", type(b) is int,
   "\n\ntype(c) is complex: ", type(c) is complex,
   "\n\ntype(country) is not float: ", type(country)
   is not float)
```

<u>Output:</u>

```
C:\Windows\system32\cmd.exe

F:\PythonScripts>python identityoperators.py
a is 3:  True
b is 7.5:  False
a is not 5:  True
type(a):  <class 'int'>
type(b):  <class 'float'>
type(c):  <class 'complex'>
type(country):  <class 'str'>
type(a) is int:  True
type(b) is int:  False
type(c) is complex:  True
type(country) is not float:  True
F:\PythonScripts>
```

Various operators will be used throughout the book. It is suggested that you try out Python scripts on your own, mixing and matching different operators. This way, you will get a practical stronghold over these concepts.

8. Interactive Python Shell

So far, whatever programs we have seen were written as Python scripts and those scripts were executed with this command – ***python <script name>***. What happens here is – the python command calls the Python interpreter which is ***python.exe*** on Windows and ***python*** binary on Linux/MAC. The ***<script name>*** is passed as a command line argument. The interpreter is designed in such a way that it fetches the contents of the mentioned script and executes it line by line. This is a standard way of writing python programs and executing them.

Interactive Python Shell offers another way of writing Python scripts but it is mostly used for rapid prototyping and testing. To launch Python Shell, open ***Command Prompt/Shell/Terminal***, type the following command and hit ***Enter***.

python

When you do not mention the script name, the Interactive Python Shell launches as shown below:

```
C:\Windows\system32\cmd.exe - python

F:\PythonScripts>python
Python 3.7.4 (tags/v3.7.4:e09359112e, Jul  8 2019, 20:34:20) [MSC v.1916 64 bit
(AMD64)] on win32
Type "help", "copyright", "credits" or "license" for more information.
>>>
```

In this shell, you can execute any python statements and it will show you the result then and there. Let us try out the following statements and see what we get:

```
print ("Inside Python Shell!")
a = 4.542
b = 8
c = 3 + 6j
name = "Rebecca"
year = 2019
print (a)
print (b)
print (c)
print (name)
print (year)
3 + 7 * 3 + 9 ** 2 - 6/4 + 342%7 - 454//5
d = a * b + c
print (d)
print (type(a))
print (type(b))
print (type(c))
print (type(d))
```

When you manually execute these statements one by one, this is what you should see:

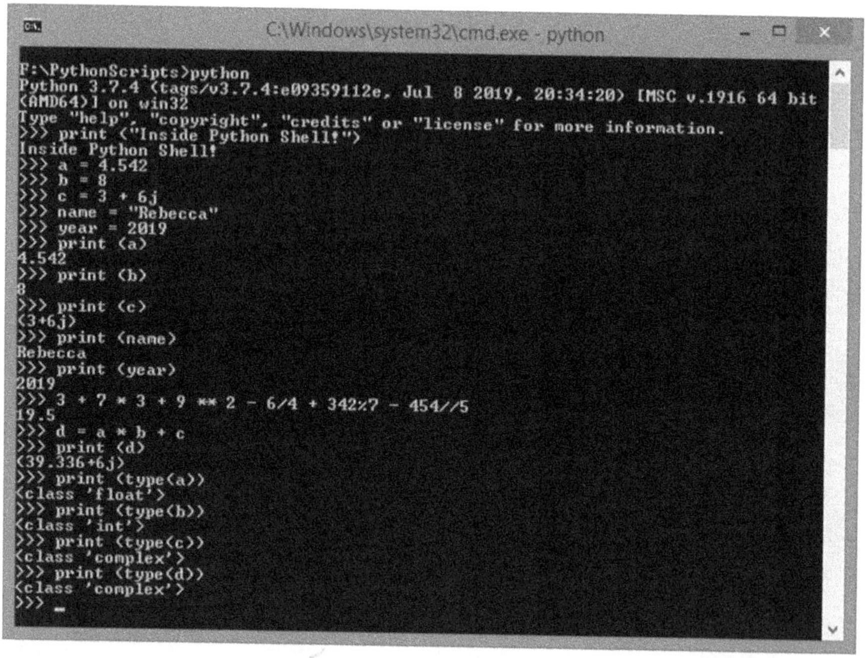

```
C:\Windows\system32\cmd.exe - python
F:\PythonScripts>python
Python 3.7.4 (tags/v3.7.4:e09359112e, Jul  8 2019, 20:34:20) [MSC v.1916 64 bit
(AMD64)] on win32
Type "help", "copyright", "credits" or "license" for more information.
>>> print ("Inside Python Shell!")
Inside Python Shell!
>>> a = 4.542
>>> b = 8
>>> c = 3 + 6j
>>> name = "Rebecca"
>>> year = 2019
>>> print (a)
4.542
>>> print (b)
8
>>> print (c)
(3+6j)
>>> print (name)
Rebecca
>>> print (year)
2019
>>> 3 + 7 * 3 + 9 ** 2 - 6/4 + 342%7 - 454//5
19.5
>>> d = a * b + c
>>> print (d)
(39.336+6j)
>>> print (type(a))
<class 'float'>
>>> print (type(b))
<class 'int'>
>>> print (type(c))
<class 'complex'>
>>> print (type(d))
<class 'complex'>
>>> _
```

As you can see, the result of the execution is shown then and there. This is a very powerful tool for rapid prototyping and testing. It is highly recommended that you keep the Interactive Python Shell open whenever you learn any new python concepts and try out the new statements that you learn inside the shell.

9. User Input

All of the concepts we have learned and scripts written so far had ***hardcoded*** variable values. In this section we will learn how to accept input from the user. The easiest way of accepting user input is using the ***input( )*** function. The basic syntax of this function is:

<variable> = input (<prompt message>)

Example:

name = input ('Enter your name: ')

When ***input(<prompt message>)*** statement is encountered, the string in ***<prompt message>*** will be displayed on the console. This is a way to prompt the user to enter something through the keyboard. When the user enters some text and presses ***Enter***, the entered text will be fetched by this function and returned to the specified ***<variable>*** in ***string format***. What are return values, how does the return process work has been covered in detail in the ***Functions*** chapter. For simplicity, let us understand the working of this function with the help of an example. Consider the following statement:

country = input('Enter your country: ')

When this statement is encountered, the execution of the script will pause until the user enters something through the keyboard and presses Enter. Say, the user has typed in ***'South Africa'*** and hit Enter. The text ***'South Africa'*** will be returned and stored in the variable ***country***. You can then make use of this variable anywhere in your program later. You can try the above statement inside the Interactive Python Shell as shown below:

```
C:\Windows\system32\cmd.exe - python
F:\PythonScripts>python
Python 3.7.4 (tags/v3.7.4:e09359112e, Jul  8 2019, 20:34:20) [MSC v.1916 64 bit
(AMD64)] on win32
Type "help", "copyright", "credits" or "license" for more information.
>>> country = input ('Enter your country: ')
Enter your country: _
```

You will notice that you have been prompted to enter some value. You may enter anything you wish. I will enter ***'Estonia'*** and display the contents and the type of the variable ***country***.

```
C:\Windows\system32\cmd.exe - python
F:\PythonScripts>python
Python 3.7.4 (tags/v3.7.4:e09359112e, Jul  8 2019, 20:34:20) [MSC v.1916 64 bit
(AMD64)] on win32
Type "help", "copyright", "credits" or "license" for more information.
>>> country = input ('Enter your country: ')
Enter your country: Estonia
>>> print (country)
Estonia
>>> print (type(country))
<class 'str'>
>>>
```

This function uses blocking I/O operation – the program will wait for the user to enter something. If the user does not enter anything, the execution will halt there indefinitely. The process will continue to run in the background until something is entered or the process is terminated externally.

Let us write a simple python script to accept different inputs from the user and display them back:

```
#Simple User Input Demo
#Prompt the user to enter name, age and address
name = input ('Enter your name: ')
```

```
age = input ('Enter your age: ')
address = input ('Enter your address: ')
#Display entered values and their type
print ("Name: ", name,
         "Address: ", address,
         "Age: ", age)
```

Output:

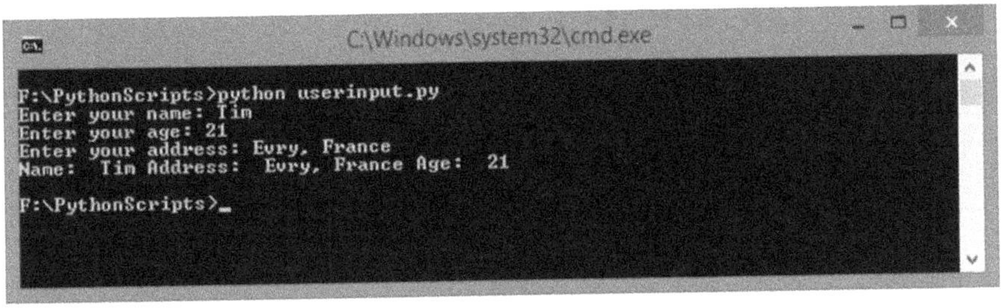

```
C:\Windows\system32\cmd.exe
F:\PythonScripts>python userinput.py
Enter your name: Tim
Enter your age: 21
Enter your address: Evry, France
Name:  Tim Address:  Evry, France Age:  21

F:\PythonScripts>_
```

The ***input()*** function always returns the entered value in a string format. This is not ideal in all cases. For example, you want to accept two numbers from a user, they will be read as strings and not as numeric data types. You will not be able to perform arithmetic operations of any kind on string data types. If you want to read numbers to perform mathematical operations, the string data type must be first converted to numeric data type. You will learn more about data type conversion in the next chapter.

10. Data Type Conversion

This chapter talks about converting data from one type to another. There are several built-in functions that help us perform data type conversion but we will be only looking at the important ones. Data type conversion is particularly useful (but not limited to) when you read data from the user. For example, if you want to read two numbers from the user and compute their sum, the ***input()*** function used to read data from the user will only give you data in the string format. In such a situation, you would first read the data as string and then convert to the numeric type using the appropriate data type conversion function. It is worth noting that not all data types can be converted to every other data type, hence appropriate care needs to be taken while performing data conversion.

10.1 Convert to Integer

Function ***int (<x>)*** is used to convert ***<x>*** to an integer. If you read a number as input from the user into ***<x>*** using the ***input()*** function, it will be a string. The ***int*** function will convert ***<x>*** to an integer and return it as an integer data type. Syntax:

<variable> = int (<x>)

Example:

data = input ('Enter a number: ')

num = int (data)

10.2 Convert to Float

Function ***float (<x>)*** is used to convert ***<x>*** to a floating point value. The ***float*** function will convert ***<x>*** to a float and return it as a float data type. Syntax:

<variable> = float (<x>)

Example:

data = input ('Enter a number: ')

num = float (data)

10.3 Convert to Complex

Function ***complex (<real>, <imaginary>)*** is used to convert ***<real>, <imaginary>*** parts into a complex number. You can also read a complex number as a string into a variable say **<x>** and pass this variable to the ***complex*** function. Syntax:

<variable> = complex (<x>)

#OR

<variable> = complex(<real>, <imaginary>)

Example:

data = input ('Enter a number: ')

c = complex (<x>)

10.4 Convert to String

You can convert almost everything to string using the ***str(<x>)*** function. Syntax:

<variable> = str (<x>)

Example:

z = 120

s = str (z)

This function will return the data in a string format.

10.5 Convert to Hexadecimal String

An integer can be converted to a hexadecimal equivalent using the ***hex(<x>)*** function. Syntax:

<variable> = hex (<x>)

Example:

x = 43

h = hex (x)

This function will return the data in a string format.

Let us write a python script to read two integer values from the user and perform various arithmetic operations. The values read using the ***input()*** functions will be of string type. We will use the ***int()*** function to convert the string values to integers.

```
#User input, arithmetic operations
#Prompt the user to enter two numbers x, y
x_str = input ('Enter an integer: ')
y_str = input ('Enter another integer: ')
#Convert x_str and y_str from string to integer
x = int (x_str)
y = int (y_str)
#Perform Arithmetic operations, assign result to
variables
#Calculate sum
sum = x + y
#Calculate difference
difference = x - y
#Calculate product
product = x * y
#Perform division
quotient = x / y
#Modulus
mod = x % y
#Perform floor division
floor_quotient = x // y
#Exponent
exp = x ^ y
#Display everything
```

```
print("\nx = ", x , "y = ", y,
     "\nsum = ", sum ,
     "\ndifference = ", difference ,
     "\nproduct = ", product ,
     "\nquotient = ", quotient ,
     "\nremainder = ", mod ,
     "\nquotient (floor value) = ", floor_quotient ,
     "\nexponent = ", exp
     )
```

Output:

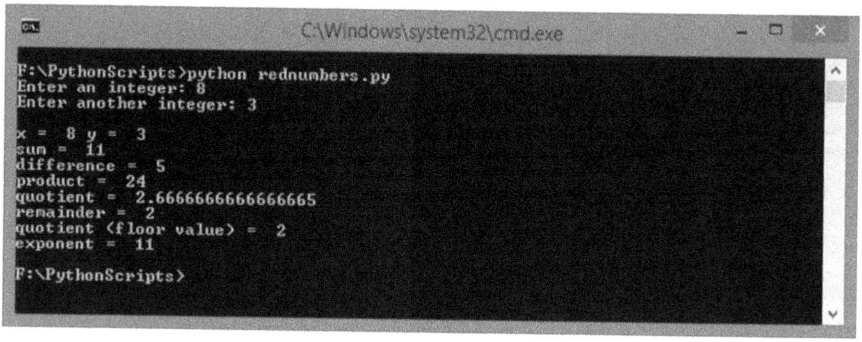

```
C:\Windows\system32\cmd.exe

F:\PythonScripts>python rednumbers.py
Enter an integer: 8
Enter another integer: 3

x =  8 y =  3
sum =  11
difference =  5
product =  24
quotient =  2.6666666666666665
remainder =  2
quotient (floor value) =  2
exponent =  11

F:\PythonScripts>
```

11. Control Structures

Control structures are programming constructs used to exercise control over the execution of a program. A python script executes in a top-down manner, statement by statement. So far, we have not seen any execution that is conditional in nature. Control structures let you set rules of execution. Python offers control structures in the form of decision making constructs and loops. All of the decision making constructs are written using blocks and hence you need to be careful about code indentations.

11.1 Decision Making

Decision making is done with the help of if-else construct.

This construct is the most basic but useful decision making tool based on whether a given condition is true or false. Let us start with a simple if-block. The general syntax of writing an if-block is:

```
if (<condition>):
    #Statements to be executed if <condition> is True
```

Example:

```
if (num % 5 == 0):
    #Statements under this if block should be at a tab-space indent
    print ("num is divisible by 5")
```

The if-block begins with ***if (<condition>):*** statement. All the statements that you want to put under this block should be at one tab-space indent from the previous indent. When the if statement is encountered the given ***<condition>*** is evaluated. The ***<condition>*** is normally an expression that evaluates to ***True*** or ***False***. If the ***<condition>*** evaluates to ***True***, the statements under the ***if-block*** (those at one tab-space indent) will be executed and if it evaluates to ***False***, the statements will not be executed.

Consider the above example cited just after the if syntax. We check if ***num*** is divisible by ***5*** using the expression ***(num % 5 == 0)***. If it evaluates to ***True***, the ***print*** statement inside the block will be executed and if not, it will be skipped.

There can be an optional else block immediately following the if block which gets executed when the given ***<condition>*** of the if statement evaluates to ***False***. General syntax of using if and else together is:

if (<condition>):

#Statements to be executed if <condition> is True

else:

#Statements to be executed if <condition> is False

Example:

if (num % 5 == 0):

#Statements under this if block should be at a tab-space indent

print ("num is divisible by 5")

else:

#Statements under this else block should be at a tab-space indent

print ("num is not divisible by 5")

When you use just if and else together, your decision making options are limited by the evaluation of just one condition. If you want to check for multiple conditions, you can use the ***elif*** construct; ***elif*** is a short for ***else-if***. You can place as many ***elif*** blocks between the ***if block*** and the ***else block***, with each ***elif*** block having their own condition. The general syntax is:

if (<condition 1>):

#Statements to be executed if <condition 1> is True

elif (<condition 2>):

#Statements to be executed if <condition 1> is False and <condition 2> is True

elif (<condition 3>):

#Statements to be executed if <condition 1> is False and <condition 3> is True …

…

elif (<condition n>):

#Statements to be executed if <condition 1> is False and <condition n> is True else:

#Statements to be executed if <condition> is False

Here is how the whole if-elif-else decision making structure works – First, the condition of the ***if block*** will be evaluated. If it evaluates to ***True***, the ***if block*** will be evaluated. We have understood this part so far. If the condition evaluates to ***False***, the ***if block*** will be skipped and the condition of the immediate ***elif*** block (if it is present) will be checked. If that condition evaluates to ***True***, the ***elif*** block will be executed. If the condition evaluates to ***False***, that ***elif*** block will be skipped and the control will jump to the next ***elif*** block (if any) and its condition will be checked. This process will go on until one of the conditions of the ***elif*** blocks evaluates to ***True***. If none of the conditions evaluate to ***True***, the ***else block*** (if it is present) will be evaluated. In one ***if-elif-else*** combination structure, only one block – either ***if*** block, or exactly one ***elif*** block or ***else*** block will be executed. For example, if the condition of the ***if block*** or that of one of the ***elif blocks*** evaluates to ***True***, that particular ***if block*** or ***elif block*** will be executed and the remaining ***elif*** blocks and ***else*** block (if present) will be skipped. Let us write a python script to read a number from the user and check if it is positive, negative or zero.

```
#Positive, negative, zero
#Prompt the user to enter a number
x_str = input ('Enter a number: ')
#Convert the input to int
num = int (x_str)
#Check if num is positive, negative or zero
#Check if num is greater than 0
if (num > 0):
    #Statements to be executed if num is greater than 0
    print ("The number: ", num, " is positive.\n")
#Check if num is less than 0
elif (num < 0):
    #Statements to be executed if num is less than 0
    print ("The number: ", num, " is negative.\n")
#If the number is neither positive nor negative, it is 0
else:
    #Statements to be executed if num is equal to 0
    print ("The number: ", num, " is zero.\n")
```

Output:

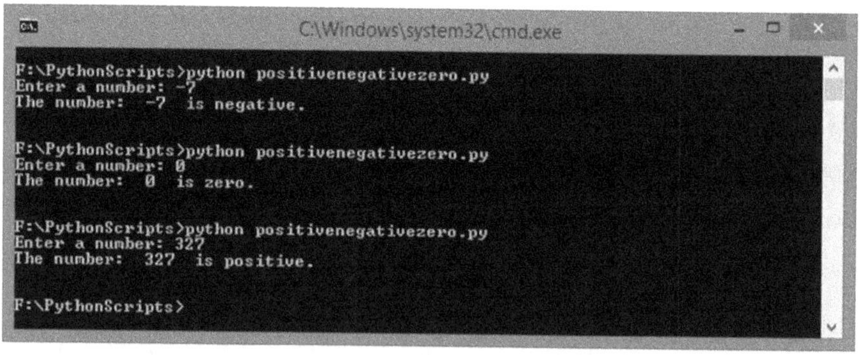

```
C:\Windows\system32\cmd.exe

F:\PythonScripts>python positivenegativezero.py
Enter a number: -7
The number:  -7  is negative.

F:\PythonScripts>python positivenegativezero.py
Enter a number: 0
The number:  0  is zero.

F:\PythonScripts>python positivenegativezero.py
Enter a number: 327
The number:  327  is positive.

F:\PythonScripts>
```

To fortify the concepts of blocks and indentations, let us take a look at the screengrab of the above script written using Notepad++:

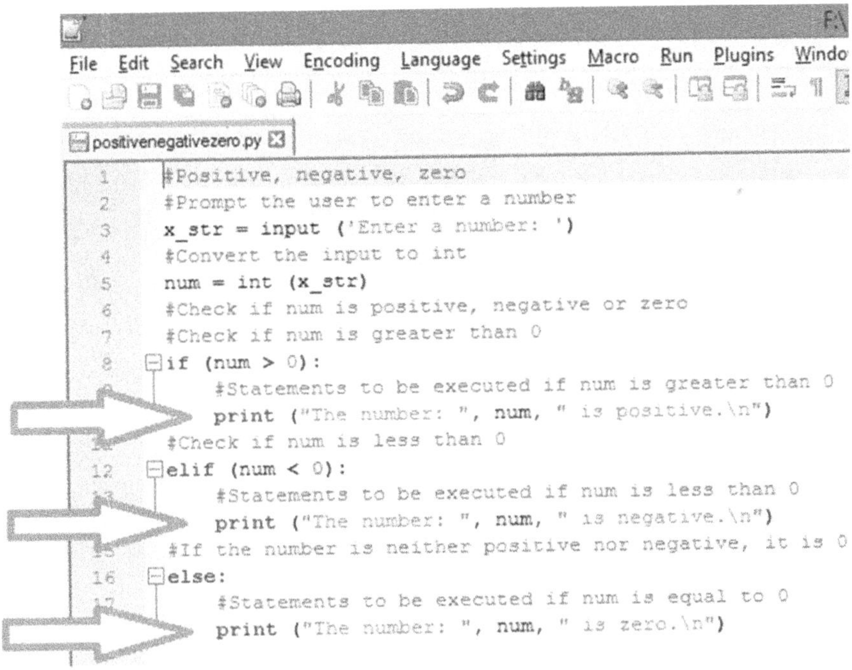

```
#Positive, negative, zero
#Prompt the user to enter a number
x_str = input ('Enter a number: ')
#Convert the input to int
num = int (x_str)
#Check if num is positive, negative or zero
#Check if num is greater than 0
if (num > 0):
    #Statements to be executed if num is greater than 0
    print ("The number: ", num, " is positive.\n")
#Check if num is less than 0
elif (num < 0):
    #Statements to be executed if num is less than 0
    print ("The number: ", num, " is negative.\n")
#If the number is neither positive nor negative, it is 0
else:
    #Statements to be executed if num is equal to 0
    print ("The number: ", num, " is zero.\n")
```

Take a look at the orange arrows, notice how exactly one tab-space indent is left under the ***if, elif and else*** statements. This is how blocks of codes are denoted in python.

11.2 Loops

Loops are used to execute a block of code over and over again as long as a condition is met. In Python, there are two loops – ***while loop*** and ***for loop***. In this chapter, we will only learn while loop and for loop will be covered in the next chapter. This is because, you need to understand strings, lists, tuples or dictionaries in order to understand for loop.

The general syntax of writing a while loop is:

while (<condition>):

#Statements...

A while loop is accompanied by a ***<condition>*** which can either evaluate to ***True*** or ***False***. If the condition evaluates to ***True***, the statements inside the while block are evaluated one by one. Once the execution reaches the end of the block, the specified condition is checked again and if it evaluates to ***True*** again, the block is executed again. This process goes on until the specified condition evaluates to ***False***. Each instance of a loop block execution is known as an ***iteration***. If the condition never evaluates to ***False***, the loop will go on executing indefinitely until the program is terminated externally. Such a loop is known as an ***infinite loop***.

Let us write a python script to display the multiples of 3 from 3 to 30 using while loop:

```
#While loop demo
#Initialize a variable to 1
i = 1
#Loop from 1 to 10
while (i <= 10):
    #Print i x 3
    print ( i * 3 )
    #Increment i
    i = i + 1
```

Output:

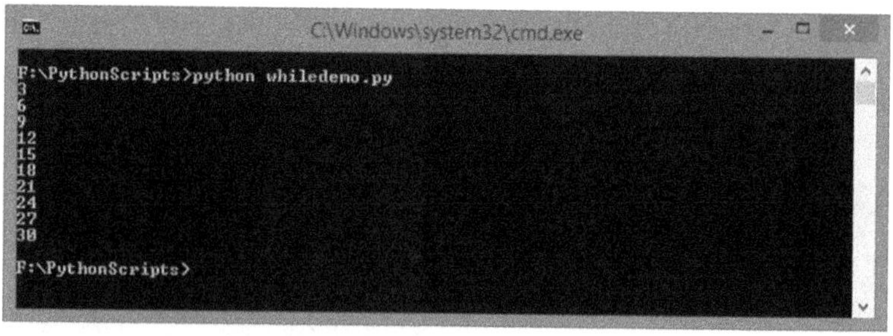

```
C:\Windows\system32\cmd.exe
F:\PythonScripts>python whiledemo.py
3
6
9
12
15
18
21
24
27
30

F:\PythonScripts>
```

In the above program, we initialize a variable called *i* to *1*. When the execution control encounters the ***while*** statement, the condition *i <= 10* is checked. When *i* is *1*, *i <= 10* will evaluate to ***True*** and the statements under the while block will be executed. Towards the end of the block, *i* is incremented by 1. Before the next iteration, the condition is checked again. Now, *i* is *2* and *i <= 10* still evaluates to ***True***. This will go on until *i* becomes *10*. When *i* becomes *11*, *i <= 10* will evaluate to ***False*** and the loop will no longer execute.

11.2.1 Control Statements

The normal procedure of loop execution is – the statements inside the loop block will go on executing as long as the specified condition evaluates to True. You can alter this process of execution using loop control statements. There are 3 control statements – ***break***, ***continue*** and ***pass***. A ***break*** statement will terminate the execution of a loop and the control will come out of the loop. A ***continue*** statement will skip the remaining statements and the control will jump to the starting of the loop, thereby carrying on with the next iteration. A ***pass*** statement does not do anything but is required syntactically; it is like no-operation (NOP). Let us learn the significance of each of these statements with the help of programming examples.

Let us write a script to print from 0 to 9 and come out of the loop when the count reaches 5. Here is how we would use the break statement:

```
#break demo
#Initialize count to 0
count = 0
#Loop from 0 to 9
while (count < 9):
    #Check if count is 5
```

```
    if (count == 5):
        #Break out of the loop if count is 5
        break
    #Print count
    print (count)
    #Increment count
    count = count + 1
```

Output:

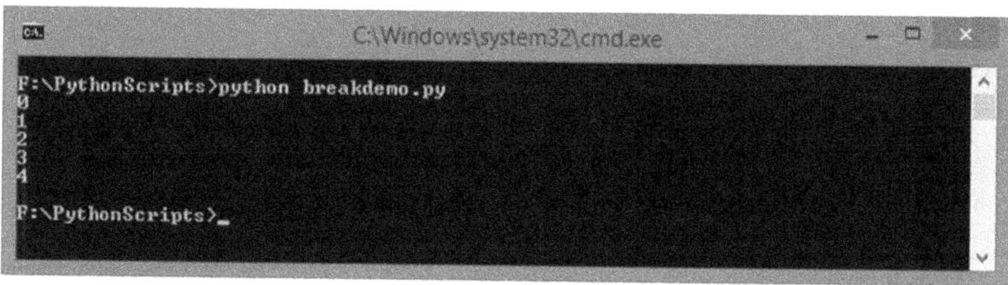

Moving on to the continue statement, let us write a python script to display the multiples of 5 between 5 and 50 but skip when the number is also a multiple of 2.

```
#continue demo
#Initialize count to 0
count = 0
#Loop from 0 to 9
while (count < 10):
    #Increment count
    count = count + 1
    #Check if count x 5 is a multiple of 2
    if ((count * 5) % 2 == 0):
        #Skip this iteration if count x 5 is a
        multiple of 2
        continue
    #Print count x 5
    print (count * 5)
```

Output:

```
C:\Windows\system32\cmd.exe
F:\PythonScripts>python continuedemo.py
5
15
25
35
45

F:\PythonScripts>
```

The control statement ***pass*** does not do anything to the execution of the loop but can be useful in certain situations. For example, we have seen how if-else works. Say, we have meaningful code to be executed only in the else block, we can include a ***pass*** statement in the if block. Let us write a program to display numbers from 1 to 15 and exclude numbers that are multiples of 3.

```
#pass demo
#Initialize count to 1
count = 1
#Loop from 1 to 15
while (count <= 15):
   #Check if count is a multiple of 3
   if (count %3 == 0):
         #Do nothing here
         pass
   else:
         #Print count
         print (count)
   #Increment count
   count = count + 1
```

Output:

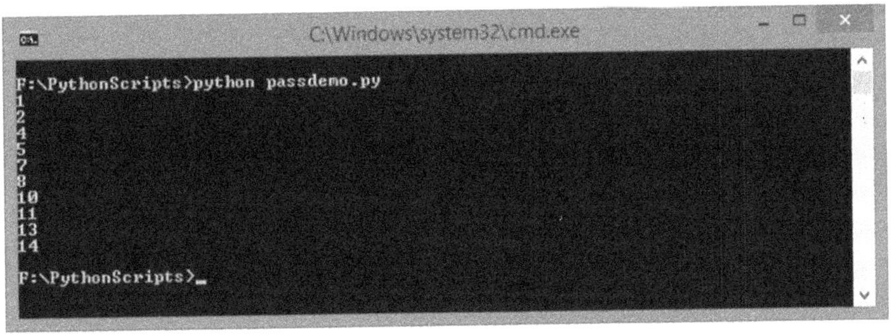

```
C:\Windows\system32\cmd.exe
F:\PythonScripts>python passdemo.py
1
2
4
5
7
8
10
11
13
14

F:\PythonScripts>_
```

12. Strings

A string is a sequence of characters. We have seen how to assign a string to a variable and how to print it. In this chapter, we will learn more details about strings.

Being a sequence of characters, each character is present at an index that runs from 0 to 1 less than the length of the string. For example, consider the following string initialization:

s_var = "Python eBook"

The above string contains 12 characters. The first character ***'P'*** is present at index *0* and the last character ***'k'*** is present at index ***11***. This is how the string would look internally:

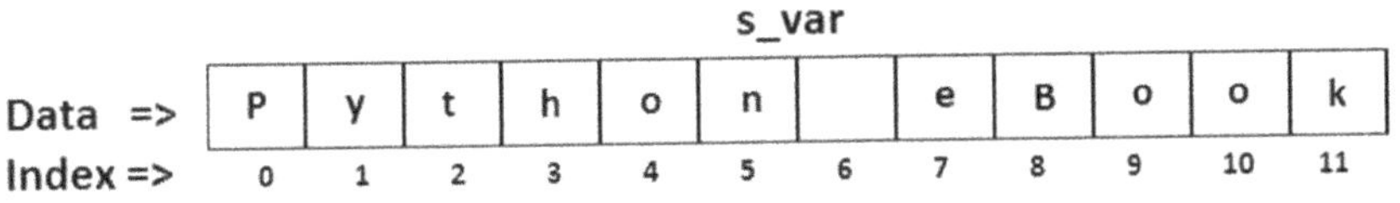

Note that space is also a character just like any other alphabet at index 6.

Individual characters of the string can be accessed with the ***slice operator ([ ])***. The general syntax is:

<variable>[<index>]

Example:

first = s_var [0]

last = s_var [11]

The last character can also be accessed using the index ***-1***.

12.1 Substring

A substring can be extracted from a main string using the ***range slice operator ([:]).*** The general syntax is:

<variable>[<start index> : <end index>]

Example:

#Characters starting from index 0 to 3

S1 = s_var [0:4]

#Characters starting from index 5 till the end of the string

S2 = s_var [5:]

#Characters starting from the start of the string till character at index 4

S3 = s_var [:3]

12.2 String Concatenation

More than one strings can be concatenated using the concatenation operator (+). The general syntax is:

<variable> = <string 1> + <string 2> + … + <string n>

Example:

s_1 = "Hello"

s_2 = "Python"

s_3 = s_1 + " " + s_2

12.3 Miscellaneous String Operations

There are many built in functions that perform various string operations. Here are a few useful ones:

12.3.1 String length

The function ***len(<string>)*** is used to find the length of the string. Example:

l = len (name)

12.3.2 Lower chase check

The function ***<string>.islower()*** is used to check if the string is in lower case. The function returns ***True*** if all the characters of the ***<string>*** are lower case, ***False*** otherwise.

12.3.3 Upper case check

The function **<string>.isupper()** is used to check if the string is in upper case. The function returns ***True*** if all the characters of the ***<string>*** are upper case, ***False*** otherwise.

12.3.4 Convert to lower case

The function ***<string>.lower()*** is used to convert the string to lower case. Example:

L_string = name.lower ()

12.3.5 Convert to upper case

The function ***<string>.upper()*** is used to convert the string to upper case. Example:

U_string = name.upper ()

Let us write a script to demonstrate some of the string concepts we learned so far:

```
#String Operations demo
#Initialize two strings
demo_str = "This is a sample string."
greeting_str = "Hello!"
#Display strings
print("String 1: ", demo_str, "Length: ",
len(demo_str),
      "\nString 2: ", greeting_str, "Length: ",
      len(greeting_str))
#Concatenate
s = greeting_str + " " + demo_str
print("\nConcatenated String: ", s, "Length: ",
len(s))
#Print different slice operation results
print("\nDifferent slice operation results:\n")
print(demo_str[5:], "\n", greeting_str[:3], "\n",
s[12:24], "\n", greeting_str[4],"\n", demo_str[2:7],
"\n" )
print("\nUpper case: ", demo_str.upper())
print("\nLower case: ", s.lower())
```

Output:

```
C:\Windows\system32\cmd.exe
F:\PythonScripts>python stringdemo.py
String 1:  This is a sample string. Length:  24
String 2:  Hello! Length:  6

Concatenated String:  Hello! This is a sample string. Length:  31

Different slice operation results:

is a sample string.
 Hel
 is a sample
 o
 is is


Upper case:  THIS IS A SAMPLE STRING.

Lower case:  hello! this is a sample string.

F:\PythonScripts>_
```

12.4 Membership Operators and Strings

There are two membership operators in Python – ***in*** and ***not in***. These can be used with strings, lists, tuples, dictionary, etc. Here, we will see how these operators can be used with strings. The ***in*** operator will tell if a character or a string is present in another string. If ***present***, it will return ***True***, if ***not present***, it will return ***False***. General syntax:

<string 1> in <string 2>

Example:

```
String1 = "States"
String2 = "United States of America"
if (String1 in String2):
        print ("\nString1 is present in String2")
```

On the other hand, the ***not in*** operator will return ***True*** if one string is ***not present*** in the other string and ***False*** otherwise. General syntax:

<string 1> not in <string 2>

Example:

```
String1 = "DC"
String2 = "United States of America"
if (String1 not in String2):
        print ("\nString1 is not present in String2")
```

12.5 For loop and Strings

In ***Control Structures*** chapter, we only learned ***while*** loop under the loops section. Let us see how a ***for*** loop works and how it will let us work with strings. The reason why ***for*** loop was not covered under Control Structures' Loops section is because this loop works only with iterative data types such as strings, lists, tuples, dictionary, etc. The general syntax of for loop with iterative data types is:

for <variable> in <iterative variable>:

#Statements…

Example:

msg = "Loops"

for var in msg:

print (var)

Consider the above example. There is a variable called ***msg*** which holds the string data ***"Loops"***. In the ***for loop statement***, the iterative variable is ***msg***. During each iteration of the loop, each character from ***msg*** will be fetched into the variable ***var*** starting with ***'L'*** up to ***'s'***. If you run the above code, this is what you will see:

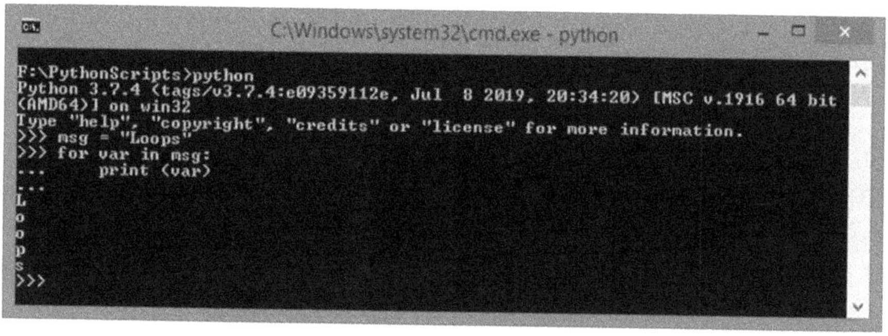

```
C:\Windows\system32\cmd.exe - python
F:\PythonScripts>python
Python 3.7.4 (tags/v3.7.4:e09359112e, Jul  8 2019, 20:34:20) [MSC v.1916 64 bit
(AMD64)] on win32
Type "help", "copyright", "credits" or "license" for more information.
>>> msg = "Loops"
>>> for var in msg:
...     print (var)
...
L
o
o
p
s
>>>
```

Each character from ***msg*** is fetched into ***var*** and then ***var*** is printed during each iteration of the for loop. Hence, we can say that the <u>number of iterations of a for loop will be equal to the number of elements present in the iterative data type if control statements are not used inside the loop</u>. In this case, there are 5 characters in the string "Loops" and the loop runs for 5 times. You can cross check it with a counter variable which is incremented during each iteration. We will modify the above code to:

```
msg = "Loops"
count = 0
for var in msg:
        print (var)
        count = count + 1
print ("Number of iterations: ", count)
```

Here is what you should see:

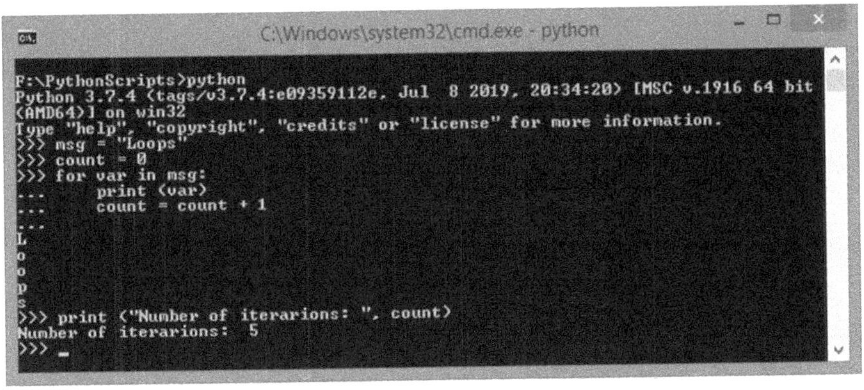

```
C:\Windows\system32\cmd.exe - python

F:\PythonScripts>python
Python 3.7.4 (tags/v3.7.4:e09359112e, Jul  8 2019, 20:34:20) [MSC v.1916 64 bit
(AMD64)] on win32
Type "help", "copyright", "credits" or "license" for more information.
>>> msg = "Loops"
>>> count = 0
>>> for var in msg:
...     print (var)
...     count = count + 1
...
L
o
o
p
s
>>> print ("Number of iterarions: ", count)
Number of iterarions:  5
>>> _
```

13. Lists and Tuples

Lists and Tuples are iterative data types. Let us look at each one of them.

13.1 Lists

A list is a collection of items of any data type. A list can be created by assigning a collection of items separated using commas, enclosed within square brackets. The general syntax of creating a list is:

<list variable> = [<item 1>, <item 2>, … <item n>]

Example:

list_x = ['Jack', 57.5, 'Brazil', 2+7j, 600]

In the above example, there is a list called ***list_x*** which contains different elements of different data types such as string, numbers and complex. The first element of the list is present at index 0 and the last element is present at 1 less than the length of the list. You can use the ***len(<list>)*** function to find the length of the list. In the above example, the first element ***'Jack'*** is present at ***index 0*** and the last element ***600*** is present at ***index 4***. Here is what the above list will look like in the memory:

list_x

Data =>	**Jack**	**57.5**	**Brazil**	**2+7j**	**600**
Index =>	**0**	**1**	**2**	**3**	**4**

13.1.1 List Operations

Individual elements of a list can be accessed with the ***slice operator ([ ])***. The general syntax is:

<list variable>[<index>]

Example:

first = list_x [0]

last = list_x [4]

The last character can also be accessed using the index ***-1.*** Elements can be updated using the index as follows:

<list_variable>[index] = <new value>

Example:

#Change Brazil at index 2 to Argentina

list_x[2] = 'Argentina'

A sub-list can be extracted from a bigger list using the ***range slice operator ([:]).*** The general syntax is:

<list *variable>[<start index> : <end index>]*

Example:

#Elements starting from index 1 to 3

l1 = x_list [1:4]

#Elements starting from index 2 till the end of the string

l2 = x_list [2:]

 # Elements starting from the start of the string till character at index 2

l3 = x_list [:3]

More than one lists can be combined together with the help of the ***concatenation operator (+)***. Syntax:

<joined list> = <list 1> + <list 2> + … + <list n>

An element from a list can be deleted using the del statement as follows:

del <list_variable> [<index>]

Example:

del x_list [3]

When an element is deleted, all the elements after the deleted element will be shifted by one place towards the left.

If you know the value of the element to be deleted, you can use the ***remove()*** function as follows:

<list variable>.remove(<element value>)

Example:

x_list.remove(2+7j)

The remove function will find the first occurrence of the item and delete it. All the elements after that item will be shifted by one place towards the left.

An item can be appended to an existing list using the ***append()*** function:

<list variable>.append(<element>)

Example:

x_list.append('Good Bye')

Let us write a python script to demonstrate some of these concepts:

```
#List Demo
#Initialize a few lists
list1 = [23, 6+9j, 'Motorola', 5.66, 'Mouse']
list2 = ['GM', -3.6, 7]
#Find lengths
l1 = len (list1)
l2 = len (list2)
#Displays lists using print and element by element using while
print ("\nList 1\n", list1)
print ("\nList 2\n", list2)
print ("\nDisplaying element by element using while\n")
i = 0
print ("\nList 1\n")
while (i < l1):
   print("Index: ", i , "Element: ", list1[i])
   i = i + 1
i = 0
print ("\nList 2\n")
while (i < l2):
   print("Index: ", i , "Element: ", list2[i])
   i = i + 1
#Concatenate
list3 = list1 + list2
print ("\nList 3\n", list3)
#Perform various slicing operations
print ("\nSlicing operations on lists\n")
print(list3[6:], "\n", list1[:3], "\n", list3[1:5], "\n", list2[2],"\n", list3[3:6], "\n" )
```

Output:

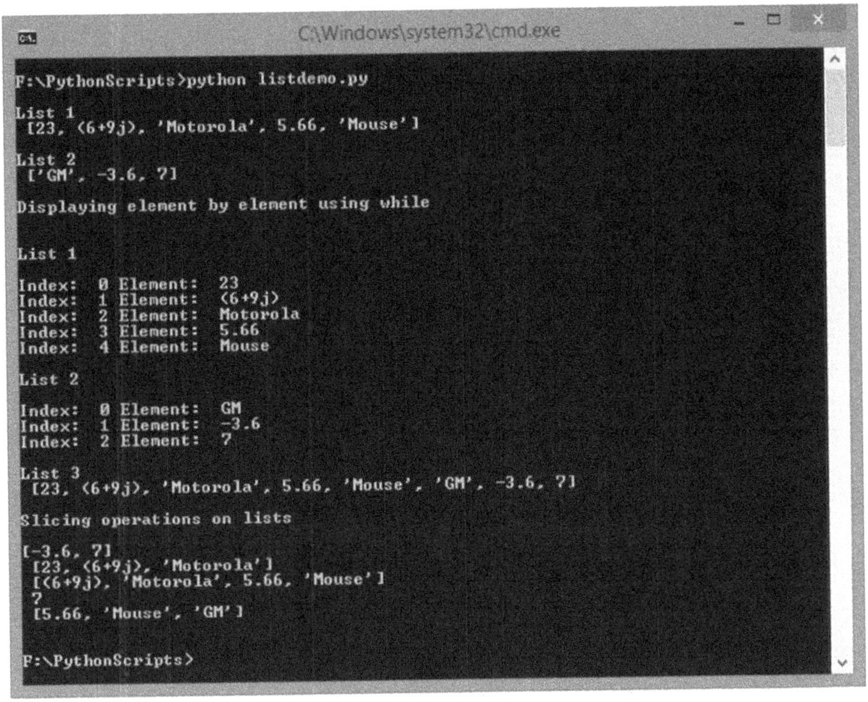

```
C:\Windows\system32\cmd.exe

F:\PythonScripts>python listdemo.py
List 1
 [23, (6+9j), 'Motorola', 5.66, 'Mouse']
List 2
 ['GM', -3.6, 7]
Displaying element by element using while

List 1
Index:  0 Element:  23
Index:  1 Element:  (6+9j)
Index:  2 Element:  Motorola
Index:  3 Element:  5.66
Index:  4 Element:  Mouse

List 2
Index:  0 Element:  GM
Index:  1 Element:  -3.6
Index:  2 Element:  7

List 3
 [23, (6+9j), 'Motorola', 5.66, 'Mouse', 'GM', -3.6, 7]
Slicing operations on lists
[-3.6, 7]
 [23, (6+9j), 'Motorola']
 [(6+9j), 'Motorola', 5.66, 'Mouse']
 7
 [5.66, 'Mouse', 'GM']

F:\PythonScripts>
```

13.2 Tuples

A tuple works just like a list but changes cannot be made to a tuple once it is formed. We can say that a tuple is a read-only list.

A tuple can be created by assigning a collection of items separated using commas, enclosed within brackets. The general syntax of creating a tuple is:

<tuple variable> = (<item 1>, <item 2>, … <item n>)

Example:

tuple_1 = (1, 2, 'Hello', 3.7, 'X', 65)

Similar to a list, the index will begin at 0 and end at one less than the size of the tuple (given by ***len(<tuple>)*** function). Individual elements of a list can be accessed with the ***slice operator ([ ])***. The general syntax is:

<tuple variable>[<index>]

Example:

first = tuple_1 [0]

last = tuple_1 [5]

The ***rang slice ([:])*** operator will work on a tuple exactly in the same way that it would on a list.

13.3 Membership Operators and Lists/Tuples

Membership operators– ***in*** and ***not in*** can be used with Lists and Tuples. The ***in*** operator will tell if an element is present in the given List/Tuple. If ***present***, it will return ***True***, if ***not present***, it will return ***False***. General syntax:

<element> in <List/Tuple>

Example:

list_1 = [1, 3, 'K']

if ('K' in list_1):

print ("\nK is present in list_1")

On the other hand, the ***not in*** operator will return ***True*** if an element is ***not present*** in the given List/Tuple and ***False*** otherwise. General syntax:

<element> not in <List/Tuple>

Example:

tuple_1 = (10, 9, 'Fox', -4.6, 2+95j)

if ('X' in tuple_1):

print ("\nX is present in tuple_1")

else:

print ("\nX is not present in tuple_1")

13.4 For loop and Lists/Tuples

Lists and Tuples are iterative data types and hence for loop can be used to traverse a list/tuple.

for <variable> in <List/Tuple>:

#Statements…

Example:

list_1 = [2.1, -5.5, 'Lanka']

for element in list_1:

print (element)

In this example, there is a list called ***list_1*** with 3 elements. During each iteration of the loop, each element starting from ***index 0*** to ***index 2*** will be fetched into the variable ***element***. If you run the above code snippet, this is what you will see:

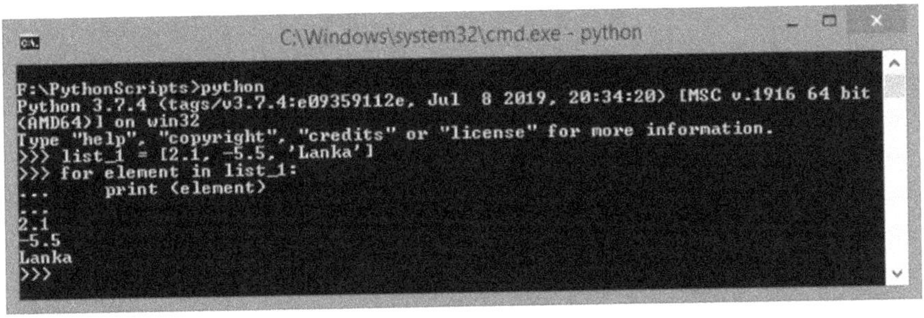

```
C:\Windows\system32\cmd.exe - python
F:\PythonScripts>python
Python 3.7.4 (tags/v3.7.4:e09359112e, Jul  8 2019, 20:34:20) [MSC v.1916 64 bit
(AMD64)] on win32
Type "help", "copyright", "credits" or "license" for more information.
>>> list_1 = [2.1, -5.5, 'Lanka']
>>> for element in list_1:
...     print (element)
...
2.1
-5.5
Lanka
>>>
```

The number of iterations a loop will go through will be equal to the number of elements present in a list/tuple if control statements are not used inside the loop.

14. Dictionary

A dictionary is a feature rich data type where data is stored in ***key-value*** pairs. In simple terms, we can refer to a key as a meaningful index. People with programming background will be able to relate a dictionary to a hash table. Keys and values could be of any data types but it makes a lot of sense to use something meaningful as a key and hence numbers and strings are preferred. A dictionary can be created by enclosing ***<key>:<value>*** pairs, separated by commas, enclosed within curly brackets. General Syntax:

> *<dictionary> = {<key 1>: <value 1>, <key 2>: <value 2>, … <key n>: <value n>}*
>
> *Example:*
>
> *person_data = {'name' : 'Karrie', 'age' : 25, 'country' : 'Norway'}*

In this example, there are 3 keys of string type – ***'name'***, ***'age'*** and ***'country'*** holding the values ***'Karrie'***, ***25*** and ***'Norway'*** respectively. You could have keys and values of literally any data types including complex number, lists, tuples, etc. But for simplicity sake, I have chosen keys of string type. This is how the dictionary ***person_data*** will look in the memory:

person_data

Values =>	Karrie	25	Norway
Keys =>	name	age	country

Technically, we could use lists or tuples to store personal data shown in this example. But, we would have to access individual elements using their numeric index. Here, we have to use keys to access elements. A dictionary is a great tool to store records and is used heavily in database programming. It must be clearer now why we can consider keys as meaningful indexes.

If you want to retrieve all the keys of a dictionary, you can use ***<dictionary>.keys()*** function, for values, you can use ***<dictionary>.values()*** function and to determine the length of the dictionary, you can use the ***len(<dictionary>)*** function.

Note: Keys have to be unique while creating a dictionary. If you use duplicate keys, the value set for the last duplicate key will be considered and previous values of that duplicate key will be lost. For example, if you create a dictionary as:

person_data = {'name' : 'Karrie', 'age' : 25, 'country' : 'Norway', 'name' : 'Sam'}

The key-value pair ***'name':'Karrie'*** will be replaced by ***'name':'Sam'***. In short, duplicate keys cannot exist in a dictionary.

14.1 Accessing a Dictionary

Data values of a dictionary can be accessed using keys as follows:

<dictionary>[<key>]
Example:
person_name = person_data ['name']
person_age = person_data['age']
person_country = person_data['country']

New key-value pair can be added to a dictionary using the following syntax:

<dictionary>[<new key>] = <value>

Example:

person_data ['occupation'] = 'Pilot'

An existing key-value pair can be updated using the same syntax:

<dictionary>[<existing key>] = <new value>

Example:

person_data ['age'] = 32

A key-value pair can be deleted using the ***del*** statement as follows:

del <dictionary>[<key>]

Example:

del person_data['country']

Once a key-value pair is deleted, the pairs after the deleted one will shift one place leftward.

14.2 Membership Operators and Dictionary

Membership operators– ***in*** and ***not in*** can be used with Dictionary. The ***in*** operator will tell if a key is present in the given Dictionary. If ***present***, it will return ***True***, if ***not present***, it will return ***False***. General syntax:

<key> in <Dictionary>

Example:

person_data = {'name' : 'Karrie', 'age' : 25, 'country' : 'Norway'}

```
if ('age' in person_data):
        print ("\nThe key - age is present in person_data")
```

On the other hand, the ***not in*** operator will return ***True*** if a key is ***not present*** in the given Dictionary and ***False*** otherwise. General syntax:

```
<key> not in <Dictionary>
Example:
person_data = {'name' : 'Karrie', 'age' : 25, 'country' : 'Norway'}
if ('occupation' not in person_data):
        print ("\nThe key – occupation is not present in
        person_data")
else:
        print ("\nThe key – occupation is present in person_data")
```

14.3 For loop and Dictionary

A for loop can be used to iterate through a Dictionary in the following way:

```
for <key> in <Dictionary>:
        #Statements
Example:
person_data = {'name' : 'Karrie', 'age' : 25, 'country' : 'Norway'}
for (key_var in person_data):
        print ("key: ", key_var, "value: ", person_data[key_var])
```

During each iteration of the loop, each key of the dictionary will be fetched into the variable ***key_var*** starting from the first key to the last one. Let us write a python script to work with a dictionary:

```
#Dictionary Demo
#Initialize a few dictionaries
employee_data = {'id' : 1023, 'name' : 'Donna',
'age' : 29}
sample_dict = {'xyz' : 534, 2+3j : 'aaa', 5.4: 425,
(1, 2, 3) : [4, 5, 6]}
print ("\nemployee_data: ", employee_data,
       "\nkeys: ", employee_data.keys(),
       "\nvalues: ", employee_data.values(),
       "\n\nsample_dict: ", sample_dict,
       "\nkeys: ", sample_dict.keys(),
       "\nvalues: ", sample_dict.values())
#Alter employee_data
#Update name
employee_data['name'] = 'Wade'
#Delete age key
del employee_data['age']
#Add country key and values
employee_data['country'] = "Australia"
#Print using for loop
print ("\nUpdated employee_data:\n")
for key_var in employee_data:
print ("Key: ", key_var, " \tValue: ",
employee_data[key_var])
```

Output:

```
C:\Windows\system32\cmd.exe

F:\PythonScripts>python dictionarydemo.py

employee_data:  {'id': 1023, 'name': 'Donna', 'age': 29}
keys:  dict_keys(['id', 'name', 'age'])
values:  dict_values([1023, 'Donna', 29])

sample_dict:  {'xyz': 534, (2+3j): 'aaa', 5.4: 425, (1, 2, 3): [4, 5, 6]}
keys:  dict_keys(['xyz', (2+3j), 5.4, (1, 2, 3)])
values:  dict_values([534, 'aaa', 425, [4, 5, 6]])

Updated employee_data:

Key:  id         Value:  1023
Key:  name       Value:  Wade
Key:  country    Value:  Australia

F:\PythonScripts>_
```

Note: When using membership operators and for loop with dictionaries, the keys of the dictionary will be iterated through and not the values directly. The values will still have to be accessed as *<dictionary>[<key>]*.

15. Functions and Modules

A function (also known as a ***method, routine or sub-routine***) is a block of code that performs a task or a group of tasks. A function is used when a block of code needs to be re-used. We have seen may built-in functions such as ***print, input, len,*** etc. So you must be having a fair idea of how to use functions. In this section, we will learn how to write our own functions and use them. ***Function definition*** and ***function call*** are two distinct things you need to learn when learning functions.

15.1 Function Definition

A function definition is the block of re-usable code that we previously talked about which performs tasks. A function is defined with the help of the ***def*** keyword. The general syntax is:

```
def <function name> ( <parameters> ):
        #Function Body
        #Statements…
        return <value>
```

Function definition can be divided into the following parts – Function Name, Parameters, Function Body, return statement.

Function Name

A function name is used to identify a function. The same rules need to be followed while naming a function as you would while naming a variable. It goes without saying that reserved keywords cannot be used to name a function.

Parameters

Parameters, also known as arguments is a list of variables that a function accepts. This is an optional field. If there are more than one parameters, they have to be separated by a comma.

Function Body

Function body is the core part of the definition where actual computational work gets gone. This part has an optional ***return*** statement which is used to return values to the calling function. Without returning any values, a ***return*** statement could be included as a good coding practice.

A function is a code block and hence the body should be present at one tab-space indent.

Here are a few examples of function definitions:

A simple function top print a message on the screen, no parameters, no return values:

```
def show_message ( ):
        print ("\nInside show_message function")
        return
```

A function that accepts 3 parameters and displays their product, does not return any data:

```
def calc_prod (int x , int y , int z ):
        print ("\nProduct: ", ( x * y * z))
        return
```

A function that accepts 2 numbers, performs division and returns the quotient:

```
def get_quotient ( a, b ):
        quotient = a / b
        return quotient;
```

15.2 Function Call

A function definition by itself will not work. It will just be a block of code sitting idle. A function needs to be called in order for the statements inside it to execute. The general syntax is:

<function name> (<parameters>)

When a function is returning a value, there must be a variable to receive the returned value. Without it, the script will be syntactically correct but the returned value will be lost. Let us call each of the functions defined in the previous section.

```
#Call show_message( )
show_message( )
#Call calc_prod, pass 3 arguments
calc_prod (4, 7.5, 2.3)
#Call get_quotient, receive the returned value in a variable
q = get_quotient (124, 9)
```

Note: The number of parameters that a function accepts in the function definition should be equal to the number of parameters passed during a function call. There is an exception to this rule when using ***default arguments*** which we will see later in this chapter.

Let us write a program where we will have 4 functions and call them one by one:

```
#Functions Demo
#Note that execution does not begin here

#display_sum definition
#Accept 3 numbers as parameters and find their sum
def display_sum(a, b, c):
    #Calculate sum of a, b and c
    sum = a + b + c
    #Display sum
    print ("\nInside display_sum\nSum = ", sum)
    #return statement, not required but a good
    programming practice
    return

#get_diff definition
#Accept 2 values, find their difference and return it
def get_diff(a, b):
    #calculate difference
    diff = a - b
    #return difference
    return diff

#get_prod definition
#Accept 3 values, find their product and return it
def get_prod(a, b, c):
    #calculate product
    prod = a * b * c
    #return product
    return prod

#get_quotient definition
#Accept 2 values, calculate quotient, return it
def get_quotient(a, b):
    #divide a by b
    q = a / b
    #return quotient
    return q

#Execution Begins Here
#Initialize some variables
x = 6
y = 4.3
z = -3
#Call the defined function one by one
display_sum(x, y, z)
diff = get_diff(x, y)
prod = get_prod(x, y, z)
```

```
    q = get_quotient(z, x)
    #Display all the values
    print ("\nOutside all functions",
        "\nDifference = ", diff,
        "\nProduct = ", prod,
        "\nQuotient = ", q)
```

Output:

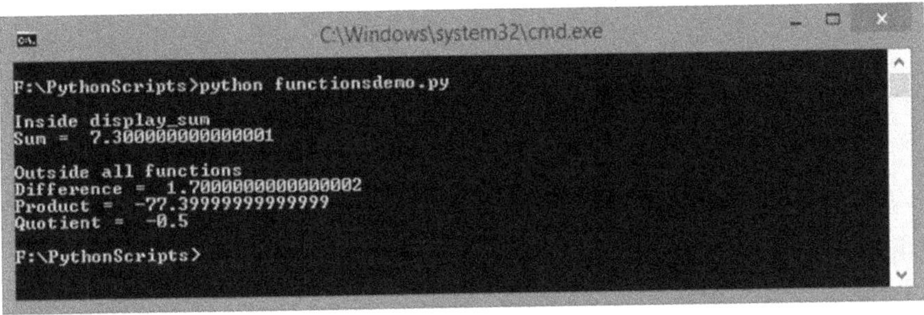

Let us take a look at how the program is written. Refer to the following screenshot:

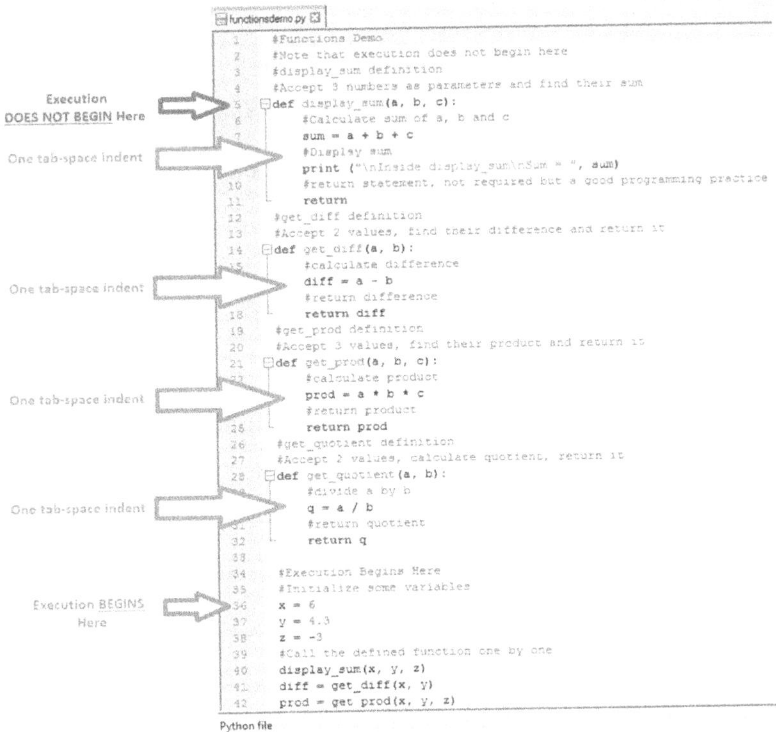

We have seen over and over again that a python script begins executing from the first statement till the last one. Here, the first meaningful statement (leaving aside comments) is ***def display_sum(a, b, c):*** at ***line number 5*** marked by the ***red arrow***. The script does not start executing from this line because this is a function block and it will remain there idle unless a call is made to this function. The execution instead begins from the statement ***x = 6*** at ***line number 36*** marked by the ***green arrow***. Also, notice how one tab-space indent is left at the beginning of each function block marked by ***orange arrows.***

15.3 Optional main function

There is a special variable in python called ***__name__***. When a script is executed using ***python <script name>*** command, this variable automatically gets the string value ***"__main__"***. This is python's internal process and the exact working is slightly more complicated than the simple explanation that has just been provided and we will stick to that. When you have multiple functions, you can check if ***__name__*** is equal to ***"__main__"*** and that ***if block*** will serve as an entry point to your script. This is a requirement only in certain situations and it will be clearly mentioned whenever such need arises through the course of this book. Otherwise, you can use the mentioned ***if block*** as an entry point to your program to make your code look well organized and clean. Alternatively, you can write your own custom main function from where you want the execution to begin and call that function from the ***if block***. Let us demonstrate this concept with the help of ***get_prod*** and ***get_diff*** function from the previous example:

```
#Optional main function Demo 1
#Note that execution does not begin here

#get_prod definition
#Accept 3 values, find their product and return it
def get_prod(a, b, c):
   #calculate product
   prod = a * b * c
   #return product
   return prod

#get_diff definition
#Accept 2 values, find their difference and return it
def get_diff(a, b):
   #calculate difference
   diff = a - b
   #return difference
   return diff

#Entry point to the script
#Check if __name__ is equal to "__main__"
#Execution Begins here
if (__name__ == "__main__"):
   x = -9
   y = -3
   z = 6.98
   #Call the defined functions one by one
   diff = get_diff(x, y)
   prod = get_prod(x, y, z)
   #Display all the values
   print ("\nInside the entry point if-block\n",
          "\nDifference = ", diff,
          "\nProduct = ", prod)
```

Output:

```
C:\Windows\system32\cmd.exe

F:\PythonScripts>python optionamaindemo1.py

Inside the entry point if-block

Difference =  -6
Product =  188.46

F:\PythonScripts>
```

As seen, the execution begins from the if-block which checks if ***__name__*** is equal to ***"__main__"***. Let us now write a custom main function, let us call it ***custom_main()***. The code under the if block will be put under this function and a call will be made to this function from the ***if block*** entry point. This will achieve the same purpose but will make the code a lot more organized:

```
#Optional main function Demo 1
#Note that execution does not begin here

#get_prod definition
#Accept 3 values, find their product and return it
def get_prod(a, b, c):
    #calculate product
    prod = a * b * c
    #return product
    return prod

#get_diff definition
#Accept 2 values, find their difference and return it
def get_diff(a, b):
    #calculate difference
    diff = a - b
    #return difference
    return diff

#Custom main function definition
def custom_main():
    x = -1.7
    y = 9
    z = -0.64
    #Call the defined functions one by one
    diff = get_diff(x, y)
    prod = get_prod(x, y, z)
    #Display all the values
    print ("\nInside custom_main() function\n",
           "\nDifference = ", diff,
           "\nProduct = ", prod)

#Entry point to the script
#Check if __name__ is equal to "__main__"
#Execution Begins here
if (__name__ == "__main__"):
```

```
#Call custom_main()
print ("\nInside if-block entry point.\n")
custom_main()
```

Output:

```
C:\Windows\system32\cmd.exe

F:\PythonScripts>python optionamaindemo2.py
Inside if-block entry point.

Inside custom_main() function
Difference =  -10.7
Product =  9.792

F:\PythonScripts>_
```

15.4 Default arguments

Default arguments are used to set default values to function parameters. When a parameter is not passed when making a function call, the default value will be considered and when it is passed, the default value will be overridden by the passed value. The general syntax of defining a function with default variables:

def <function name> (<parameter> = <default value>):

#Statements

Example:

def func1 (a, b, c = 50):

print (a, b, c)

#____#

#Function call, override default argument

Func1 (1, 4, 6)

#Function call, use default argument

Func1 (5, 7)

Note: You can have as many default arguments as you want but the default arguments should be consecutive and be placed at the end of the arguments list. A default argument cannot appear in the middle of the argument list. For example, the following snippet is correct:

Function_1 (a, b, c, d = 5, g = 7, h = 8):

<u>The following example is incorrect:</u>

Function_2 (a, b, c = 2, d, f = 9, g = 6):

Let us write a function called ***area*** which can calculate the area of a rectangle as well as the area of a circle. We know that the area of a rectangle is given by the following formula:

$$Area = length\ x\ width$$

To compute the area of a rectangle, we need to pass two arguments to a function and get their product. Area of a circle is given by the following formula:

$$Area = \pi\ x\ radius^2$$

We can break this formula down as:

$$Area = radius\ x\ radius\ x\ \pi$$

We need to pass 3 arguments to a function and get their product which will give us the area of a circle. To take care of the rectangle case, we can set the third argument to a default value of 1 and in case of a circle, we can pass the third argument as π (consider 3.14) which will override the default value of 1. Here is the code:

```
#Default Arguments
#Two mandatory parameters, 1 default variable
def area (x, y, z = 1):
    #Calculate area
    area = x * y * z
    return area
```

```
radius = 2
length = 6
width = 9
#Find area of circle as radius x radius x pi
#Override default value of z (set to 1) by pi = 3.14
area_circle = area(radius, radius, 3.14)
#Find area of rectangle
#Pass length and width, two arguments only
area_rectangle = area(length, width)
print ("\nCircle:\n",
       "\nRadius: ", radius,
       "\nArea: ", area_circle,
       "\n\nRectangle:\n",
       "\nLength: ", length,
       "\nWidth: ", width,
       "\nArea: ", area_rectangle)
```

Output:

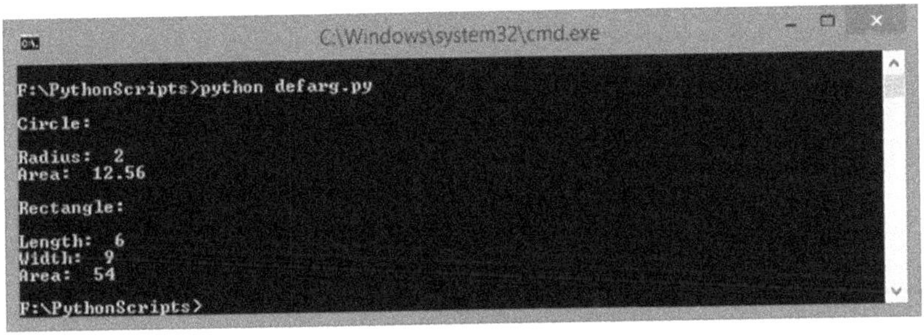

```
C:\Windows\system32\cmd.exe
F:\PythonScripts>python defarg.py
Circle:

Radius:  2
Area:  12.56

Rectangle:

Length:  6
Width:  9
Area:  54
F:\PythonScripts>
```

We could have written two different functions to calculate the area of two difference geometrical shapes. But we just wrote one function which calculates the area of two different shapes. This is a very interesting and a useful feature of functions. Try extending this function to more geometrical shapes.

15.5 Returning multiple values

A function can return more than one values. At the time of the function call, multiple variables need to be separated by comma to receive the returned values. The values will be received in the order that they are returned. Consider the following code snippet:

```
#Function Definition
def calc(a, b):
    #Calculate sum, difference, product and quotient
    s = a + b
    d = a - b
    p = a * b
    q = a / b
    #Return sum, difference, product and quotient
    return s, d, p, q
#Function call
#Values will be received in the order they are returned
sum, diff, prod, quo = calc (10, 20)
```

15.6 Modules

A module is a python file that contains definitions of functions, classes and variables. Python comes with a rich set of built-in libraries made available using modules. Built-in modules are present in different locations on different operating systems and are best left untouched. User defined modules can be placed in the local directory where the main python script is present. In order to use a module in a script, it needs to be imported with the ***import*** statement. Syntax:

```
import <module 1>, <module 2>, … <module n>
Example:
import sys
import datetime, json, re
import os
```

The above statement will import all the functions, variables and classes. If you want to import only specific components of a module, you can use the ***from*** statement:

from <module> import <component 1>, … <component n>

Example:

from os import system

Here is a script that makes use of a few functions from different modules:

```
#Modules Demo
#Import os and math
import os
import math
#Perform mathematical functions
fact = math.factorial(5)
sin_x = math.sin(2 * math.pi / 3)
#Find current working directory using os module
cwd = os.getcwd()
#Display everything
print("\nWorking directory: ", cwd,
        "\nFactorial (5): ", fact,
        "\nSin (2 x (pi / 3)): ", sin_x)
```

<u>Output:</u>

```
C:\Windows\system32\cmd.exe
F:\PythonScripts>python modulesdemo.py

Working directory:  F:\PythonScripts
Factorial (5):  120
Sin (2 x (pi / 3)):  0.8660254037844387

F:\PythonScripts>
```

Now, let us see how user defined modules work. This can be explained in the simplest possible way by putting user defined functions in one file, import that file as a module in another script. To do this, let us recall the functions we had defined in ***Section***

15.2. We will only write the functions and not the main executable code:

```
def display_sum(a, b, c):
        #Calculate sum of a, b and c
        sum = a + b + c
        #Display sum
        print ("\nInside display_sum\nSum = ", sum)
        #return statement, not required but a good
        programming practice
        return

#get_diff definition
#Accept 2 values, find their difference and return
it
def get_diff(a, b):
        #calculate difference
        diff = a - b
        #return difference
        return diff

#get_prod definition
#Accept 3 values, find their product and return it
def get_prod(a, b, c):
        #calculate product
        prod = a * b * c
        #return product
        return prod

#get_quotient definition
#Accept 2 values, calculate quotient, return it
def get_quotient(a, b):
        #divide a by b
        q = a / b
        #return quotient
        return q
```

Let us save this file as ***ourmodule.py***.

We will write another python script, let us call it ***testmodule.py*** wherein we will use functions from ***ourmodule.py***. Both the scripts should be present in the same directory. We first need to import the module file using ***import ourmodule*** statement and then access individual functions with the dot operator. For example, if we want to call ***get_quotient***, we will have to use this statement – ***ourmodule.get_quotient(2, 5)***. Here is the script:

```
#User Defined Module Demo
#Import ourmodule.py
import ourmodule
#Initialize some variables
x = 5
y = 7
z = -3
#Call functions from ourmodule
ourmodule.display_sum(x, y, z)
diff = ourmodule.get_diff(x, y)
prod = ourmodule.get_prod(x, y, z)
quo = ourmodule.get_quotient(x, y)
#Display everything
print ("\nInside testmodule.py\n\nDifference = ",
diff,
         "\nProduct = ", prod,
         "\nQuotient = ", quo)
```

<u>Output:</u>

```
C:\Windows\system32\cmd.exe
F:\PythonScripts>python testmodule.py
Inside display_sum in ourmodule.py
Sum =  9
Inside testmodule.py
Difference =  -2
Product =  -105
Quotient =  0.7142857142857143
F:\PythonScripts>
```

There are four functions in ***ourmodule.py*** and ***import ourmodule*** statement will fetch all the functions. If you want only a select few, you can use ***from <module> import <components>*** statement. Say, you are only interested in ***display_sum and get_diff*** functions, you can use ***from ourmodule import display_sum, get_diff*** statement and call the functions directly by their names without using ***ourmodule.<function>***. This is because, you have specifically mentioned what components of the module you are going to use in the ***from-import*** statement. Here is what the script will look like with selective import.

```
#User Defined Module Demo
#Fetch select function from ourmodule
from ourmodule import display_sum, get_diff
#Initialize some variables
x = 5
y = 7
z = -3
#Call functions from ourmodule
#No need to use ourmodule.<function>
display_sum(x, y, z)
diff = get_diff(x, y)
#Display everything
print ("\nInside testmodule.py\n\nDifference = ", diff)
```

Output:

```
C:\Windows\system32\cmd.exe
F:\PythonScripts>python testmodule2.py
Inside display_sum in ourmodule.py
Sum =  9
Inside testmodule.py
Difference =  -2
F:\PythonScripts>_
```

Notes:

1. When using user defined modules, the modules and the main script that executes should be placed in the same directory.
2. When using from-import statement, the select components that are imported should be referred to directly using the component name and not using ***module.<component>***.
3. It is advisable to place all the import/from-import statements at the beginning of the script.

16. Introduction to Classes and Objects

The concept of Classes and Objects come under ***Object Oriented Programming (OOP)***. Python is an object oriented scripting language and thus supports OOP. However, Object oriented programming is a huge topic and covering even a significant amount of it is beyond the scope of this book. This section is largely theoretical where we will learn the basics of object oriented programming concepts just enough to proceed further as the GUI programming chapters of this book rely on OOP concepts.

A ***class*** is a custom data type which is a collection of ***variables*** known as ***data members or properties*** and ***functions*** that operate on these data members known as ***member functions***. It is merely a definition of how this custom data type looks internally and may or may not contain data on its own.

An ***object*** is an instance of a class which has its own set of ***data members/properties*** and ***member functions*** as defined in the class. ***Data members*** are also referred to as ***Attributes***.

Let us understand the concept of classes and objects with the help of an example. Consider a ***class Employee***. What properties would we need to store the details of employees? An employee can have a ***name, age, gender, address, etc***. The class Employee will have these properties as ***data members***. We do not have any data yet; this is just the definition of the custom data type. When we create objects of his class, each object will have its own copy of ***name, age, gender, address, etc***. In layman's terms, you could refer to each object as one employee.

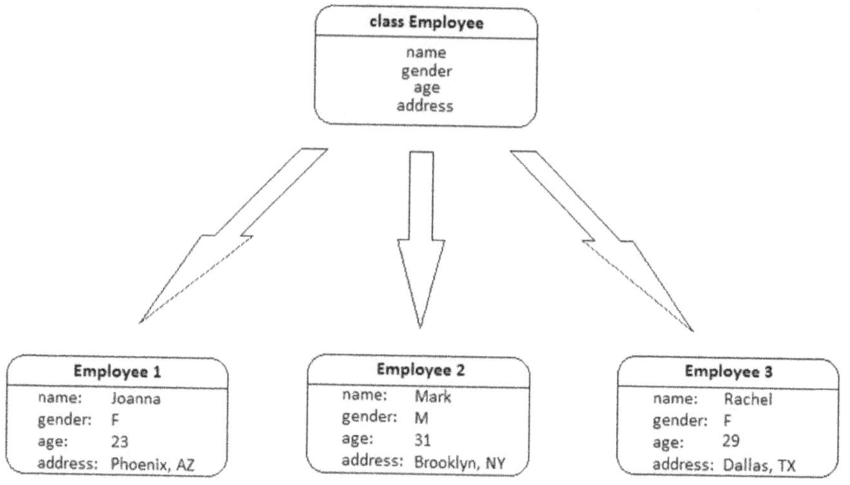

Take a look at the above diagram. The ***class Employee*** is defined with ***four data members***. Three objects – ***Employee 1, Employee 2 and Employee 3*** are created (of type Employee). Each of these 3 objects have their own copies of the 4 data members as defined in the class.

This is a very simple example which explains classes and objects with distinction. Other than data members, a class can also have functions (called member functions) which can be used to access the class' data members. For example, there could be a member function called ***getData()*** which can be used to fetch each of the attributes of an object or a function called ***setData()*** which can be used to set attributes of objects.

In addition to these elementary OOP concepts, here are a few things you should know:

Instantiation: The process of creating an object.

Constructor: A member function which gets invoked the moment an object is created. A constructor is used to initialize objects. Inside the class definition, a constructor is defined using this name - ***__init__(<parameters>)*** and called using the class name. For example – ***Employee (<parameters>)***.

Static members: Normally, an object will have its own set of data members as defined in the class. Static members are common for all objects.

Inheritance: A new class can be derived from an existing one using a process called inheritance. This enables us to preserve properties of an existing class and also saves the trouble of re-writing a new class from scratch.

Polymorphism: Polymorphism in OOP means the ability to take more than one form. In Python, polymorphism is achieved using function overloading. Meaning, a function with the same name can do different things.

16.1 Declaring your own classes

A class is declared with the help of ***class*** keyword as follows:

```
class <Class name>:
        #Data Members
        #Constructor
        #Member functions
```

Example:

```
class Person:
        name = ""
```

address = ""

age = 0

The definition of a class is done in a block of code and hence the statements inside a class should be at a tab-space indent.

Objects of a class can be declared as follows:

<obj> = <Class Name>()

Example:

P1 = Person ()

From outside the class definition (perhaps in the main routine), the attributes of an object (data members defined in the class definition) can be accessed as follows:

<obj>.<data member>

Example:

P1 = Person ()

P1.name = "Sophie"

P1.age = 41

Let us take a simple example wherein we will define a class with a few data members, create object of that class in main and access attributes of each of the objects.

```
#Class demo
class Employee:
    id = 0
    name = ''
    address = ''

if (__name__ == "__main__"):
    #Create objects of Employee
    e1 = Employee()
    e1.id = 1
    e1.name = "Dawson"
```

```
e1.address = "Manhattan"
e2 = Employee()
e2.id = 2
e2.name = "Lee"
e2.address = "Brooklyn"
#Display Everything
print (e1.id, e1.name, e1.address)
print (e2.id, e2.name, e2.address)
```

Output:

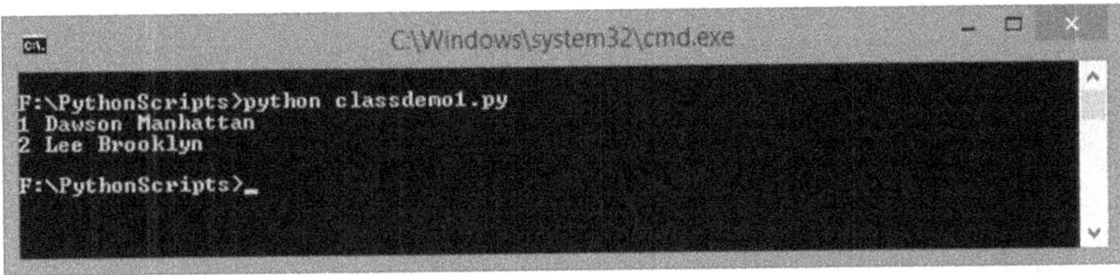

While this code does the job, data members are usually not accessed directly from outside the class. It is generally not a good programming practice. Member functions are written to access data members.

16.1.1 Member functions

Member functions are written within the class definition. These are like any other functions that we studied in ***Chapter 15*** with one major difference – every member function inside the class will have a mandatory parameter called ***self*** if you want to access the data members. An object of a class is used to call a member function. During a function call, a reference of that object is implicitly passed and is received in the ***self*** parameter. Inside the function definition, ***self.<data member>*** statement is used to access the attributes of that particular object. Let us take an example. We shall modify the code from the previous example, define two functions – ***setData()***

and ***getData()*** to set and retrieve data of an Employee object respectively.

```
#Employee class definition
class Employee:
        #Function to set attributes of an object
        #self is the mandatory parameter
        #Other parameters will be passed during
        function call
        def setData(self, id, name, address):
                self.emp_id = id
                self.emp_name = name
                self.emp_address = address
        #Function to get attributes of an object
        #self is the mandatory parameter
        def getData(self):
                return self.emp_id, self.emp_name,
                self.emp_address

if (__name__ == "__main__"):
        #Create objects of Employee
        x = Employee()
        y = Employee()
        #Set attributes of each of the objects
        x.setData(201, "Perry", "Cape Town")
        y.setData(202, "Langer", "Perth")
        #Retrieve attributs of each of the objects
        e1_id, e1_name, e1_address = x.getData()
        e2_id, e2_name, e2_address = y.getData()
        #Display Everything
        print (e1_id, e1_name, e1_address)
        print (e2_id, e2_name, e2_address)
```

<u>Output:</u>

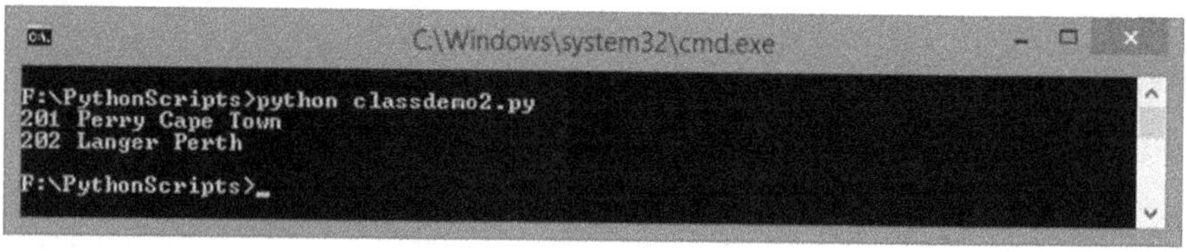

```
C:\Windows\system32\cmd.exe

F:\PythonScripts>python classdemo2.py
201 Perry Cape Town
202 Langer Perth

F:\PythonScripts>_
```

16.1.2 Constructor

A constructor is a member function of a class having the name ***__init__***. This is a special kind of a member function that is used to initialize objects. A constructor gets invoked when an object is created. Appropriate parameters should be passed during object creation for initialization. For example, if your constructor definition is as follows:

class car:

def __init__ (self, model, make, cc):

self.model = model

self.make = make

self.cc = cc

Then, you need to pass 3 arguments during object creation as follows:

c1 = car ("Audi" "Q3", 2000)

c2 = car ("BMW", "720d", 3000)

Let us modify the previous script to initialize objects using a constructor.

```
#Constructor demo
class Employee:
        #Constructor function to initialize objects
        #self is the mandatory parameter
        #Other parameters will be passed during object
        creation
        def __init__(self, id, name, address):
                self.emp_id = id
                self.emp_name = name
                self.emp_address = address
        #Function to get attributes of an object
        #self is the mandatory parameter
        def getData(self):
```

```
            return self.emp_id, self.emp_name,
            self.emp_address
if (__name__ == "__main__"):
        #Create objects of Employee and initialize
        x = Employee(550, "Eddie", "Tokyo")
        y = Employee(675, "Kayla", "Edmonton")
        #Retrieve attributs of each of the objects
        e1_id, e1_name, e1_address = x.getData()
        e2_id, e2_name, e2_address = y.getData()
        #Display Everything
        print (e1_id, e1_name, e1_address)
        print (e2_id, e2_name, e2_address)
```

<u>Output:</u>

```
C:\Windows\system32\cmd.exe

F:\PythonScripts>python constructordemo.py
550 Eddie Tokyo
675 Kayla Edmonton

F:\PythonScripts>
```

17. Introduction to GUI Application Development

Graphical User Interface (GUI) Applications are everywhere. We interact with such applications on a daily basis on desktops, mobile phones, web, etc. Back in the day when graphics technologies were not developed enough, people used to interact with the system through command line applications. As time went by, computer graphics started evolving and the need for graphics based applications also started growing. In general, GUI applications are developed using GUI frameworks – for example, .NET framework provides a rich set of features for developing GUI applications.

Whatever concepts we have learned so far, we learned to write command line applications in Python which had no graphical user interface. This chapter onward, we will learn to build GUI applications in Python.

GUI Frameworks

A GUI framework consists of a set of tools, classes, functions or a combination of all these things. There are many GUI frameworks available today. Some of the widely used ones include ***.NET framework, Tk, GTK, Qt, wxWidgets, Swing (Java), JavaFx (Java), etc.*** GUI frameworks that are native to one particular programming language are usually made available for other languages using ***language binding*** (also known as ***wrapper***). A language binding is an ***API*** (application programming interface) which allows the use of libraries written in a different language. The programmer may or may not have any knowledge of the programming language which is used to build the libraries in question. For example, there is an image processing library called ***OpenCV*** written in ***C/C++***. There is a Python wrapper for OpenCV called ***opencv-python*** using which you can make full use of the OpenCV library in Python without having to write C/C++ code.

Python distribution includes ***Tkinter*** which is a Python binding for the GUI framework ***Tk*** (written in ***C***). In a way, we can say that Tkinter is the de-facto option of building GUI applications using Python. However, this framework is very basic and not as widely used as some of the other frameworks out there.

GTK is another GUI framework written in C, widely used for developing applications for ***X11 windowing systems***. There is a python binding called ***PyGTK*** with which GTK applications can be developed using Python.

The most used stable GUI application development framework is Qt (pronounced as cute). ***PyQt*** and ***PySide*** are python bindings for Qt. We will be learning how to build GUI applications using ***PyQt***.

Qt Framework

Qt is a cross platform GUI application development framework written in C++. Qt applications can run natively on Windows, Linux, macOS, Android and embedded systems. Applications being native in nature, there is no compromise with speed and performance. Qt was first developed by a company ***Trolletech*** in 1999; the company was then acquired by ***Nokia*** in 2008. Over the years, different companies owned this framework. As of 2019, Qt framework is owned, developed and maintained by a company called ***The Qt Company***.

Qt is available under commercial and free licences (GPL, GPL 2.0, GPL 3.0, LGPL 2.1 and LGPL 3.0). Various desktop, embedded and mobile environments such as ***KDE Plasma, LXQt, Lumina, Asteroid OS, LuneOS, Sailfish OS, webOS, etc.*** are developed using Qt. Some of the well-known software applications developed in Qt include – ***Autodesk Maya, VLC Media Player, Teamviewer, Telegram, Google Earth, Virtual Box, etc.***

Being native to C++, a developer has to know C++ in order to develop Qt applications. Such applications are sometimes referred to as Qt C++ applications. However, Qt framework is made available for other languages using language bindings/wrappers. Some of the widely used Qt wrappers for programming languages other than C++ are – ***PySide (Official Qt Wrapper for Python), PyQt (for Python), Rust-Qt (for Rust), QtSharp/Qt.NET (for C#.NET), etc.***

In order to develop GUI applications using PyQt, we need to learn the basics of Qt architecture, but not necessarily Qt C++. There are two major versions of Qt – Qt4 and Qt5. We will be learning Qt5.

PyQt

As we have seen earlier, PyQt is a Qt binding for Python. With this, we can build Qt applications in Python without having to write code in C++ which is the native programming language of Qt framework.

PyQt is developed and maintained by Riverbank Computing and is available under paid as well as free licensing models. PyQt4 (no longer supported) is the binding for Qt4 and PyQt5 is the binding for Qt5. Python 2 supports Qt4 and Python 3 supports Qt5.

Install PyQt5

Installing PyQt5 will not install a full copy of Qt but binary wheels of GPL version of PyQt will include LGPL version of Qt.

We will be using a utility called ***pip*** which comes bundled with the Python distribution. The ***Python 3*** version of this utility is called ***pip3***. Open Command Prompt/Shell/Terminal, enter the following command:

pip3 install pyqt5

The installation process will begin with downloading of the required files and you should see something like this:

```
C:\Windows\system32\cmd.exe - pip3 install pyqt5

F:\>pip3 install pyqt5
Collecting pyqt5
  Downloading https://files.pythonhosted.org/packages/8f/b9/d3f2445c320274f8e19a
10f9ff9cf9fa2debdabe3c5d120c23474592f162/PyQt5-5.13.1-5.13.1-cp35.cp36.cp37.cp38
-none-win_amd64.whl (49.8MB)
    4% |█                               | 2.3MB 182kB/s eta 0:04:21
```

This may take a few minutes. Once PyQt5 is installed successfully, you will see a message as shown below:

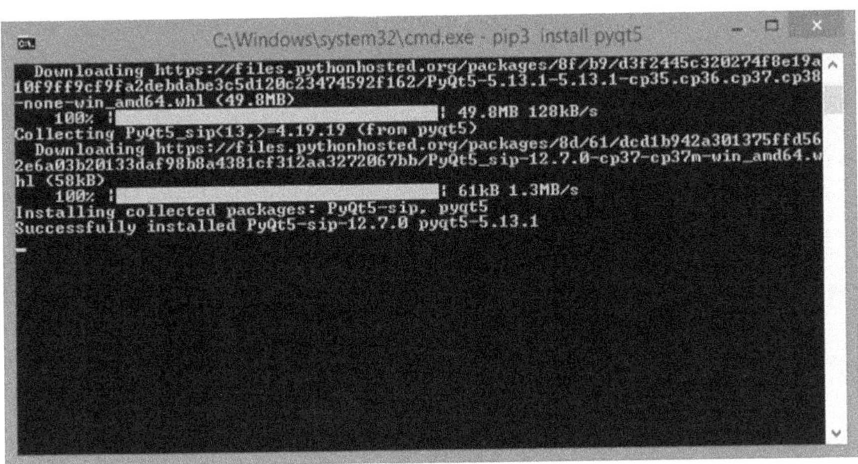

In order to make sure that PyQt5 has been successfully installed, we'll write a Python script which makes use of this binding to launch a GUI window. Copy-paste the following python code and save it as a python script with *.py* extension:

```
import sys
from PyQt5.QtWidgets import QApplication, QWidget
app = QApplication(sys.argv)
w = QWidget()
w.resize(250, 250)
w.move(300, 300)
w.setWindowTitle('Hello From PyQt')
w.show()
sys.exit(app.exec_())
```

Execute this python script as you would execute any other python script:

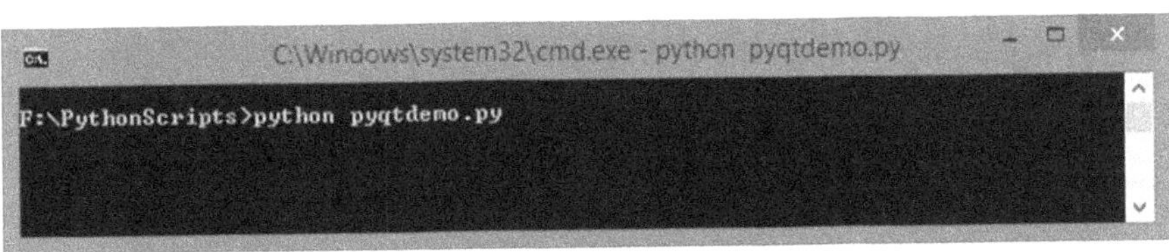

You should see a window launch like this:

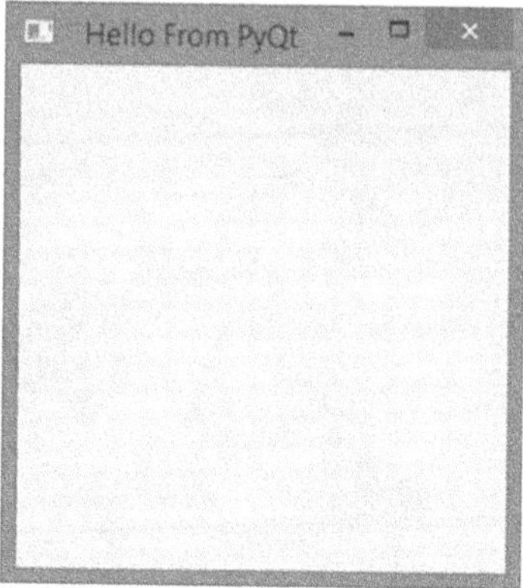

If you see this window, you have successfully installed PyQt5 and it is working fine. You do not have to understand anything that the above code does for now, we will be learning these concepts one by one.

The next step is to install ***pyqt5-tools***. This is needed because it includes a tool called ***Qt Designer*** which can be used to design GUIs in the simplest drag and drop manner. Use the following command:

pip3 install pyqt5-tools

You should see something like this:

```
C:\Windows\system32\cmd.exe
F:\>pip3 install pyqt5-tools
Collecting pyqt5-tools
  Using cached https://files.pythonhosted.org/packages/20/8e/c5ee7dcf8168327bb6d
2e3f830edadc91485f23049afaa709a3e019d47ef/pyqt5_tools-5.13.0.1.5-cp37-none-win_a
md64.whl
Requirement already satisfied: pyqt5==5.13.0 in c:\python\lib\site-packages (fro
m pyqt5-tools) (5.13.0)
Collecting click (from pyqt5-tools)
  Using cached https://files.pythonhosted.org/packages/fa/37/45185cb5abbc30d7257
104c434fe0b07e5a195a6847506c074527aa599ec/Click-7.0-py2.py3-none-any.whl
Collecting python-dotenv (from pyqt5-tools)
  Using cached https://files.pythonhosted.org/packages/57/c8/5b14d5cffe7bb06bedf
9d66c4562bf90330d3d35e7f0266928c370d9dd6d/python_dotenv-0.10.3-py2.py3-none-any.
whl
Requirement already satisfied: PyQt5_sip<13,>=4.19.14 in c:\python\lib\site-pack
ages (from pyqt5==5.13.0->pyqt5-tools) (12.7.0)
Installing collected packages: click, python-dotenv, pyqt5-tools
Successfully installed click-7.0 pyqt5-tools-5.13.0.1.5 python-dotenv-0.10.3
You are using pip version 19.0.3, however version 19.3.1 is available.
You should consider upgrading via the 'python -m pip install --upgrade pip' comm
and.

F:\>
```

Go to Python's installation directory, navigate to ***\Lib\site-packages\pyqt5_tools\Qt\bin*** and locate a file called ***designer.exe***. This is the executable file which launches ***Qt Designer***. Go ahead and execute it. ***Qt Designer*** should launch and you should see something like this:

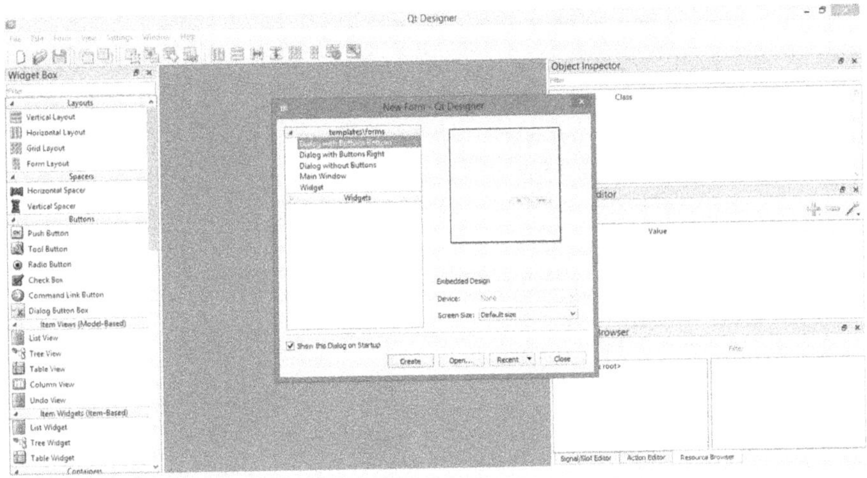

If you see this, you have successfully installed ***pyqt5-tools*** and ***Qt Designer*** is working fine.

18. Getting started with PyQt

Now that we have the required tools in place, let us learn how to build a basic *PyQt* application step by step from scratch.

18.1 User Interface (UI) Design

In Qt, user interface is designed using ***QML – Qt Modelling Language***. QML is a user interface markup language, syntactically similar to ***XML, CSS and JSON***. Learning QML is beyond the scope of this book. We shall use ***Qt Designer*** (supplied with ***pyqt5-tools***) with which we can design GUIs in a simple drag-and-drop manner.

18.1.1 Using Qt Designer

Open Qt Designer on your system. On the start-up screen, check ***Dialog without Buttons*** and click ***Create*** as shown below:

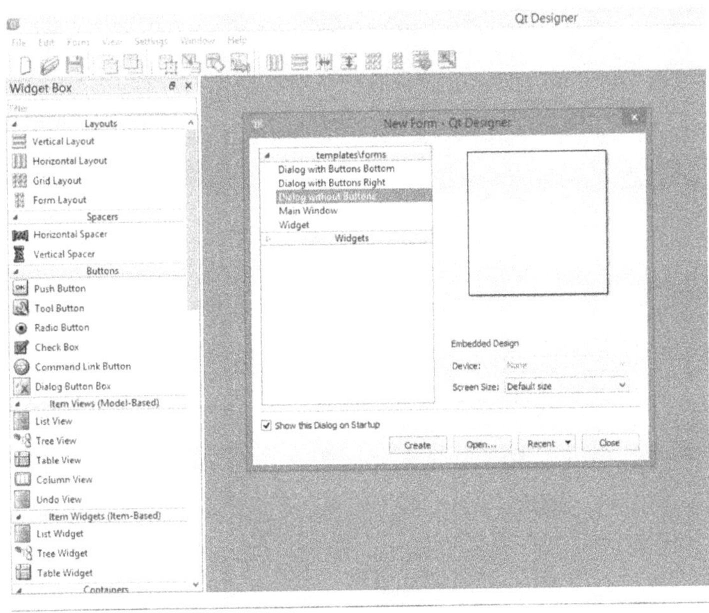

A ***Dialog window*** will be created and you will see something like following image. The important and useful parts of ***Qt Designer*** have been marked:

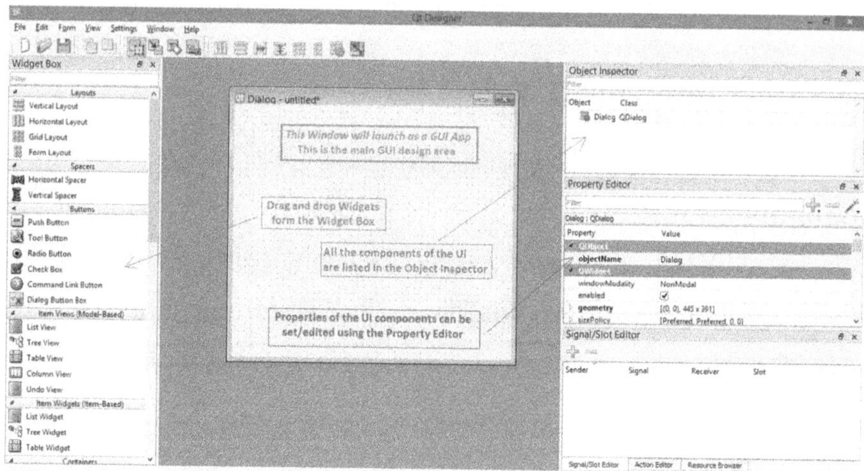

Dialog is your main UI. It is an empty application window. There is a ***Widget Box*** on the left from where you will drag and drop UI widgets like labels, buttons, text boxes, etc. There is an ***Object Inspector*** which lists all the components of your application – whatever you have included in the application – dialogs, windows, buttons, text fields, etc. ***Property Editor*** is an important box where you will set/change the properties of UI components. If you do not see any of these boxes, click ***View*** from the menu bar and check appropriate boxes.

Drag and drop any widgets of your choice on to the ***Dialog*** just to be comfortable with this feature. Let your window look messy and meaningless:

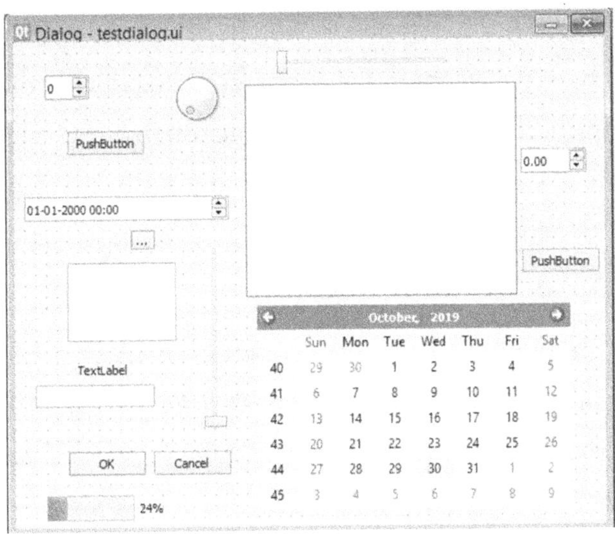

Go to ***File > Save*** and save this file at a convenient location. Notice that the extension is ***.ui***. Open this file in ***Notepad++***. You should see something like this:

testdialog.ui

```
<?xml version="1.0" encoding="UTF-8"?>
<ui version="4.0">
 <class>Dialog</class>
 <widget class="QDialog" name="Dialog">
  <property name="geometry">
   <rect>
    <x>0</x>
    <y>0</y>
    <width>559</width>
    <height>439</height>
   </rect>
  </property>
  <property name="windowTitle">
   <string>Dialog</string>
  </property>
  <widget class="QPushButton" name="pushButton">
   <property name="geometry">
    <rect>
     <x>50</x>
     <y>80</y>
     <width>75</width>
     <height>23</height>
    </rect>
   </property>
   <property name="text">
    <string>PushButton</string>
   </property>
  </widget>
```

This is ***QML*** code (you do not have to understand it) auto generated by Qt Designer. This code contains details of each and every component that you used while creating your GUI. Someone who knows QML can directly write such a code and skip using Qt Designer. Whenever you make changes to your UI and save the file, this QML code will be updated.

Let us see how to change the properties of ***Dialog***. Clear the UI by deleting all the widgets or simply go to ***File > Close and/or File > New***. Click on the title bar of the ***Dialog*** or select ***Dialog*** under ***Object Inspector***. You will see that the properties of this dialog window are listed under ***Property Editor***. There are many properties, what matters to us is ***objectName*** and ***windowTitle***. Other properties will be covered as and when required. The property ***objectName*** is used to uniquely identify the object in the UI as well as in the Python code and ***windowTitle*** is used to set the text on the title tar of the window. You may change these properties to whatever you prefer.

18.2 First PyQt Application

Let us create a new UI and use it to learn the process of building a PyQt app. We shall create an application to display ***Hello World*** text inside a window. Close all the open projects and create a new ***Dialog without Buttons*** UI in Qt Designer. Select ***Dialog*** from ***Object Inspector*** and change the properties of this window in the ***Property Editor*** box. Let the object name be Dialog for simplicity sake; set the ***Window Title*** to ***Hello World***. Under ***Widget Box > Display Widgets***, drag and drop ***Label*** on to the ***Dialog***. ***Label*** is a widget that is used to display text. Click on the label and you will see the ***Property Editor*** box now has the properties of this UI component. Scroll down and locate ***text*** property. Set the text to ***"Hello World!!!"***. You can click the small button next to the text box if you want to format the text this label is going to display. You can optionally set the ***Object Name*** of the label to something meaningful like ***label_helloworld*** as it is a good programming practice. However, we will not work with this label programmatically in this case and hence we will keep the Object Name as it is. This is what my UI looks like:

Save this file as ***helloworld.ui*** at a convenient location.

The UI file generated by Qt Designer is meaningless in Python because the UI file is written in QML which Python cannot understand. The QML code needs to be converted to Python equivalent code where each UI component will be a Python object. To do this, there is a utility called ***pyuic5*** shipped with ***pyqt5-tools*** package.

General syntax of converting QML UI to PyQt5/Python equivalent:

> *pyuic5 [QML UI] > [PyQt5/Python UI Equivalent]*
> *Example:*
> *pyuic5 testapp.ui > testapp.py*

Note: If you are unable to find ***pyuic5*** command, it is likely that the PATH variable has not been set or ***pyqt5-tools*** have not been installed properly.

In our case, let us convert the ***helloworld.ui*** file to ***helloworld_ui.py*** using the following ***pyuic5*** command:

> *pyuic5 helloworld.ui > helloworld_ui.py*

Open the ***helloworld_ui.py*** file in ***Notepad++***, this is what you will see:

helloworld_ui.py

```
# -*- coding: utf-8 -*-

# Form implementation generated from reading ui file 'helloworld.ui'
#
# Created by: PyQt5 UI code generator 5.13.0
#
# WARNING! All changes made in this file will be lost!


from PyQt5 import QtCore, QtGui, QtWidgets


class Ui_Dialog(object):
    def setupUi(self, Dialog):
        Dialog.setObjectName("Dialog")
        Dialog.resize(400, 300)
        self.label = QtWidgets.QLabel(Dialog)
        self.label.setGeometry(QtCore.QRect(80, 80, 241, 101))
        self.label.setObjectName("label")

        self.retranslateUi(Dialog)
        QtCore.QMetaObject.connectSlotsByName(Dialog)

    def retranslateUi(self, Dialog):
        _translate = QtCore.QCoreApplication.translate
```

We only need this class name

This code is auto generated by ***pyuic5*** utility when a ***.ui*** file is converted to python equivalent UI file. This code is meaningless to us; all we need to do is find the UI class, beginning with ***Ui_*** as marked in the image above. In this case, it is ***Ui_Dialog***. Notice that the ***objectName*** was set to ***Dialog*** in Qt Designer and in this file, it is prefixed with ***Ui_***. What has happened over here is, the ***pyuic5*** utility has created a class for our UI which contains the details of all the components of the UI. For example, it will contain the window title, window size, text of the label, location of the label, etc. If you could write this code directly, there would have been no need to use ***pyuic5*** command. But again, writing Qt UI code in Python is a huge topic and beyond the scope of this book and hence we will stick to designing our UIs in Qt designer and converting them to Python equivalent UI code using ***pyuic5***.

Now comes the tricky part where you will have to make use of a skeleton code for all your applications. Here is the code:

PyQt5 App Skeleton Code

```
import sys
from PyQt5.QtWidgets import QDialog, QApplication
from <python ui file> import <ui_class>

#Create a class for the application window
class <dialog window name> (QDialog):
    #Constructor function
    def __init__(self):
        #Call super-class constructor
        super().__init__()
        #Initialize and setup UI
        self.ui = <ui_class>()
        self.ui.setupUi(self)
        #Make UI Visible
        self.show()
```

```
#Main routine
if (__name__ == "__main__"):
    #Create an application instance of QApplication
    type
    app = QApplication(sys.argv)
    #Create an app window
    appwindow = <dialog window name> ()
    #Show the app window using show() function
    appwindow.show()
    #Keep the script active until the app closes
    sys.exit(app.exec_())
```

In every application that you develop, all you have to do is make changes to the underlined statements. You will make the changes as follows:

<python ui file> - UI file generated by ***pyuic5***. In our case, ***helloworld_ui.py***

<ui_class> - UI class within the python ui file beginning with *Ui_*. In our case, it is *Ui_Dialog*.

<dialog window name> - Class name for your app dialog window. You can give any unique name as you would for any variable. Let us modify this skeleton to launch the Hello World dialog window:

```
import sys
from PyQt5.QtWidgets import QDialog, QApplication
from helloworld_ui import Ui_Dialog

#Create a class for the application window
class HelloWorldDialog(QDialog):
    #Constructor function
    def __init__(self):
            #Call super-class constructor
        super().__init__()
            #Initialize and setup UI
        self.ui = Ui_Dialog()
        self.ui.setupUi(self)
            #Make UI Visible
        self.show()
```

```
if (__name__ == "__main__"):
    #Create an application instance of QApplication
    type
    app = QApplication(sys.argv)
    #Create an app window
    appwindow = HelloWorldDialog()
    #Show the app window using show() function
    appwindow.show()
    #Keep the script active until the app closes
    sys.exit(app.exec_())
```

Save this file as start_helloworld.py and run this script, the dialog window will launch as shown:

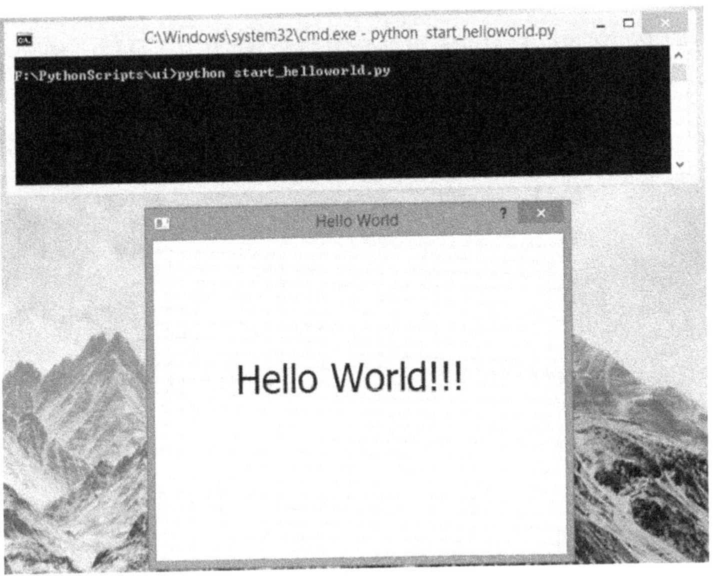

Let us recap the procedure to design and launch PyQt apps:

Step 1: Open Qt Designer, start a new project, select ***Dialog without Buttons.***

Step 2: Design the desired UI, drag and drop widgets from the ***Widget box***, change properties of the components wherever necessary, set appropriate ***objectName*** for each object. Save the project to a ***.ui*** QML file.

Step 3: Convert the ***.ui*** file to PyQt UI equivalent using ***pyuic5*** command:

pyuic5 [.ui QML file] > [pyqt/python ui file]

Step 5: Open the Python/PyQt5 UI file and determine the UI class name which will be prefixed by ***Ui_***. This will be the ***objectName*** of the ***Dialog*** box from ***Qt Designer*** prefixed with ***Ui_***. For example, if your ***Dialog*** box was called ***MyDialog***, the UI class name will be ***Ui_MyDialog***.

Step 6: Refer to the PyQt5 App Skeleton Code, copy it to a new python file and replace ***<python ui file>, <ui_class> and <dialog window name>*** appropriately. Save the python script and execute it.

Notes:

1. In Qt Designer, the property ***objectName*** is very important as it is used to uniquely identify UI components.
2. Whenever you make changes to the UI inside Qt Designer, only the .ui file will be updated and not the PyQt/Python equivalent file. Hence, you will have to run the ***pyuic5*** command to generate the PyQt/Python equivalent file every time you make changes to the UI and save it in Qt Designer.
3. The PyQt/Python file contains merely the UI definitions and cannot execute on its own. Do not try to execute this script as it does not have a main routine. Another python script should be created with the PyQt5 App Skeleton Code and this script should be executed.

19. Widgets

Widgets are UI elements such as label, button, text boxes, etc. If you take a look at the Widget box in Qt Designer, you will find all the available widgets. Each widget will have a set of properties. Covering each and every widget and their properties is beyond the scope of this book. Let us learn about a few important widgets and some of their properties. We will see show to access their properties programmatically. When you set the ***objectName*** of a widget inside ***Qt Designer***, an object of that Widget class type having the same name as ***objectName*** is created in the ***PyQt/Python UI file*** after running the ***pyuic5*** command. This code is automatically generated inside the ***setupUi*** member function under the UI class (beginning with ***Ui_***). You will almost never have to touch this code, just use it for reference.

Inside the PyQt5 App Skeleton Code – under class ***<dialog window name>*** (QDialog) , there is a constructor. In that constructor, we create a UI object of UI class type called ***ui*** using the statement -- self.ui = ***<ui_class>()*** . Since this object is of the UI class type (as defined in the PyQt/Python script), it can access all the UI elements. To access any UI element, you will use the following statement:

self.ui.<ui element's objectName>

Example:

self.ui.pushButton

self.ui.label

Properties of the UI elements are accessed using member functions of the appropriate class as follows:

self.ui.<ui element's objectName>.<function> ( )

Example:

self.ui.label.setText("Hello World")

name = self.ui.lineEdit.getText( )

Let us take a look at some of the widgets and their properties. The real significance of this section will be clearer in the next chapters where we are going to deal with events. Over here, we are only learning how to work with different widgets and their properties.

19.1 Label

A label is used to display text. The text of a label widget can be retrieved using the ***text( )*** function as follows:

text = <label object>.text ( )

Example:

text = self.ui.label1.text ( )

Text can be set using the ***setText ( )*** function as follows:

<label>.setText (<string>)

Example:

self.ui.label.setText ("Hello World!!!")

19.2 Line Edit

A Line Edit is an input widget. It is like a text box where a user can enter text. Whatever text is present in this box can be retrieved using the ***text ( )*** function:

text = <line edit object>.text ()

Example:

text = self.ui.lineEdit1.text ()

Text can be set using the ***setText ()*** function as follows:

<line edit object>.setText (<string>)

Example:

self.ui.lineEdit.setText ("Sample Text")

19.3 Plain Text Edit

This is another input widget like Line Edit but usually meant for a bigger chunk of text. Whatever text is present inside Plain Text Edit box can be retrieved using the ***getPlainText ()*** function:

text = <plain text edit object>.getPlainText ()

Example:

text = self.ui.plainTextEdit.getPlaintext ()

Text can be set using the ***toPlainText ()*** function as follows:

<plain text edit object>. toPlainText (<string>)

Example:

self.ui. plainTextEdit.toPlainText ("Lots of text")

19.4 Combo Box

A Combo Box is a drop down box which can contain a collection of items. You can programmatically add or remove items – ***addItem ()*** function is used to add new item to the combo box as follows:

<combo box object>.addItem (<item>)

Example:

self.ui.comboBox.addItem ("USA")

self.ui.comboBox.addItem ("Canada")

An item can be removed using its index (which starts at 0) as follows:

<combo box object>.removeItem (<index>)

Example:

self.ui.comboBox.removeItem (1)

self.ui.comboBox.removeItem (0)

The text of the selected item can be retrieved using the ***currentText ()*** function as follows:

selected_item_text = <combo box object>.currentText ()

Example:

selected_item_text = self.ui.comboBox1.currentText ()

19.5 Check Box

A check box is a selection based UI widget. You can check if a check box is checked using the ***isChecked ()*** function:

<check box object>.isChecked ()

Example:

self.ui.checkBox_1.isChecked ()

If the check box is checked, the ***isChecked ()*** function will return ***True***, Otherwise will return ***False***.

The display text of a check box can be retrieved using the ***text ()*** function:

<check box object>.text ( )

Example:

self.ui.checkBox_1.text ( )

19.6 Radio Button

A radio button is a selection based UI widget just like a check box but with one major difference – only one radio button from a group of radio button can be checked at a given time; if you check another one, the previous radio button will be unchecked and the new one will be checked. Radio Buttons are usually grouped inside a ***Group Box*** (container widget) because, if they are not, you will not be able to use another set of radio buttons anywhere in your window as you will only be able to check one button at a time. You can check if a radio button is checked using the ***isChecked ( )*** function:

<radio button object>.isChecked ( )

Example:

self.ui.radioButton_1.isChecked ( )

If the radio button is checked, the ***isChecked ( )*** function will return ***True***, Otherwise will return ***False***.

The display text of a radio button can be retrieved using the ***text ( )*** function:

<radio button object>.text ( )

Example:

self.ui.radioButton_1.text ( )

19.7 List Widget

A list widget is an item widget used to store a collection of items. This differs from a combo box in many ways – while combo box is a drop down box which upon clicking reveals the list of items; whereas, a list widget is a rectangular box which displays the item collection. You can add a new item to a list widget using the ***addItem ()*** function as follows:

<list widget object>.addItem (<item>)

Example:

self.ui.listWidget.addItem ("Motorola")

self.ui.listWidget.addItem ("LG")

Multiple items can be selected and the selected items can be retrieved using the function ***selectedItems ()*** :

<list widget object>.addItem (<item>)

Example:

items = self.ui.listWidget.selectedItems ()

The ***selectedItems ()*** function returns a list of items which can be iterated through using a ***for*** loop. Even if only one item is selected, this function will still return a list with only one item in it.

Note: Always give meaningful names to widgets. For example, if you have a ***lineEdit*** to take name as an input, it makes sense to name that widget as ***lineEdit_name*** as opposed to something like ***lineEdit_1***.

20. Event Handling using Signals and Slots

Event handling is a critical part of GUI application development. Every GUI application development framework has its own mechanism of handling events. In Qt and PyQt, events are handled using ***Signals and Slots***.

A ***Signal*** is emitted when an event occurs. An event can be anything such as a button click, text changed inside a Line Edit, item changed in a combo box, etc. A ***Slot*** is a function that is called to handle a particular event. For example, when a button is clicked, there will be a function designated to perform certain tasks when this click event occurs.

The coding for ***Signals and Slots*** should happen in the ***main executable script*** (derived from PyQt5 App Skeleton Code) and not in the PyQt5/Python UI equivalent script (although possible, but this file is best left unedited). ***Slot*** functions should be defined inside the main class, should have a mandatory parameter ***self***. ***Signals*** should be ***connected*** to ***Slots*** inside the constructor of the same class (***__init__*** function) after the ***self.ui.setupUi(self)*** statement. The general syntax of connecting a signal to a slot is:

self.ui.<ui element>.<signal>.connect (self.<slot function>)

Let us take a look at a few important events.

20.1 Button Click

When a ***PushButton*** is clicked, it emits a signal called ***"clicked"***. If you had a button called ***pushBotton_submit*** and you wanted to invoke a function called ***pushButton_submit_clicked*** every time the user clicks on the button, here is how you would connect this signal and slot:

self.ui.pushButton_submit.clicked.connect (self.pushButton_submit_clicked)

Let us build a PyQt application with two ***Line Edit*** widgets and one ***Push Button***. When the ***Push Button*** is clicked, we will copy the text from the first ***Line Edit*** to the second one and also print the text into the terminal. This is how our UI will look like:

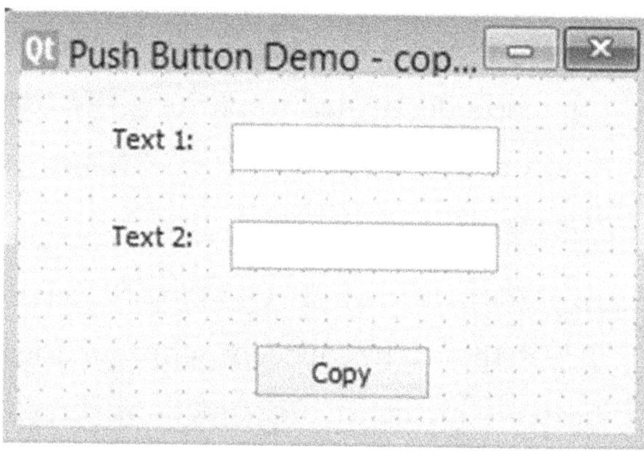

We have a dialog box with 2 ***labels***, 2 ***line edits*** and one ***push button***. Ignore the labels, focus on the important UI elements. We have seen in ***Section 19.2*** how to retrieve text from a ***Line Edit***. First line edit has been named as ***lineEdit_src***, the second one as ***lineEdit_dest*** and the pushButton as ***pushButton_copy***.

Let us now convert this QML UI to PyQt5/Python script using the ***pyuic5*** command. Let us name it ***copytext_ui.py***. Here is how this script would look like:

```
# -*- coding: utf-8 -*
# Form implementation generated from reading ui file
'copytext.ui'
```

```
# Created by: PyQt5 UI code generator 5.13.0
# WARNING! All changes made in this file will be lost!

from PyQt5 import QtCore, QtGui, QtWidgets

class Ui_Dialog(object):
    def setupUi(self, Dialog):
        Dialog.setObjectName("Dialog")
        Dialog.resize(261, 145)
        self.label = QtWidgets.QLabel(Dialog)
        self.label.setGeometry(QtCore.QRect(40, 20,
        47, 13))
        self.label.setObjectName("label")
        self.label_2 = QtWidgets.QLabel(Dialog)
        self.label_2.setGeometry(QtCore.QRect(40, 60,
        47, 13))
        self.label_2.setObjectName("label_2")
        self.lineEdit_src =
        QtWidgets.QLineEdit(Dialog)
        self.lineEdit_src.setGeometry(QtCore.QRect(90,
        20, 113, 20))
        self.lineEdit_src.setObjectName("lineEdit_src")
        self.lineEdit_dest =
        QtWidgets.QLineEdit(Dialog)
        self.lineEdit_dest.setGeometry(QtCore.QRect(90
        , 60, 113, 20))
        self.lineEdit_dest.setObjectName("lineEdit_des
        t")
        self.pushButton_copy =
        QtWidgets.QPushButton(Dialog)
        self.pushButton_copy.setGeometry(QtCore.QRect(
        100, 110, 75, 23))
        self.pushButton_copy.setObjectName("pushButton
        _copy")

        self.retranslateUi(Dialog)
        QtCore.QMetaObject.connectSlotsByName(Dialog)

    def retranslateUi(self, Dialog):
        _translate = QtCore.QCoreApplication.translate
        Dialog.setWindowTitle(_translate("Dialog",
        "Push Button Demo"))
        self.label.setText(_translate("Dialog", "Text
        1:"))
        self.label_2.setText(_translate("Dialog",
        "Text 2:"))
        self.pushButton_copy.setText(_translate("Dialo
        g", "Copy"))
```

Let us create the main script derived from PyQt5 App Skeleton Code to launch our UI. Inside the main class, we will write a slot function called ***pushButton_copy_clicked***. This function will copy the text from ***lineEdit_src*** to ***lineEdit_dest***. Inside the constructor, we will connect the "***clicked***" signal to this slot function as follows:

self.ui.pushButton_copy.clicked.connect (self.pushButton_copy_clicked)

Here is the full script (***start_copytext.py***):

```
import sys
from PyQt5.QtWidgets import QDialog, QApplication
from copytext_ui import Ui_Dialog

#Create a class for the application window
class CopyTextDialog(QDialog):
    #Slot to handle pushButton_copy's click event
    def pushButton_copy_clicked(self):
        #Fetch text from the first line edit
        text = self.ui.lineEdit_src.text()
        #Print on the terminal
        print ("Button clicked!\nText: ", text)
        #Copy to the second line edit
        self.ui.lineEdit_dest.setText(text)
    #Constructor function
    def __init__(self):
#Call super-class constructor
        super().__init__()
        #Initialize and setup UI
        self.ui = Ui_Dialog()
        self.ui.setupUi(self)
        #Connect pushButton_copy's clicked signal to
        pushButton_copy_clicked
    self.ui.pushButton_copy.clicked.connect(self.pushB
    utton_copy_clicked)
        #Make UI Visible
        self.show()
#Main routine
if (__name__ == "__main__"):
    #Create an application instance of QApplication
    type
    app = QApplication(sys.argv)
```

```
#Create an app window
appwindow = CopyTextDialog()
#Show the app window using show() function
appwindow.show()
#Keep the script active until the app closes
sys.exit(app.exec_())
```

When you run this script, the UI will launch. Enter some text in the first line edit field and click ***Copy***. Notice what happens in the terminal and also in the second line edit:

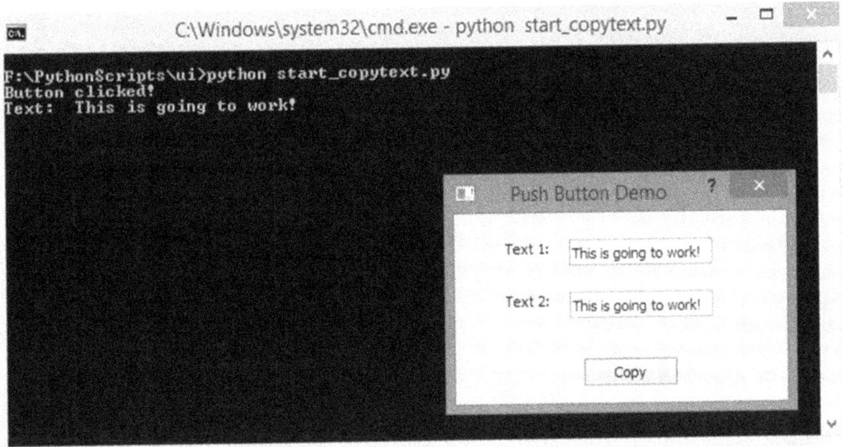

20.2 Text Changed

When the text inside input widgets such as ***lineEdit***, ***textEdit*** and ***plainTextEdit*** is changed, a signal called ***"textChanged"*** is emitted. If you had a ***lineEdit*** called ***lineEdit_message*** and wanted to invoke a function called ***lineEdit_message_changed*** every time the user made changes to the text, here is how you would connect the signal and the slot:

> *self.ui.lineEdit_message.textChanged.connect(self.lineEdit_message_changed)*

Let us build a PyQt application to copy text from a ***lineEdit*** to a ***plainTextEdit*** on the fly without the help of a click event. Whenever the user makes changes to the text inside the ***lineEdit***, it should be reflected inside the ***plainTextEdit***. Here is what the UI looks like:

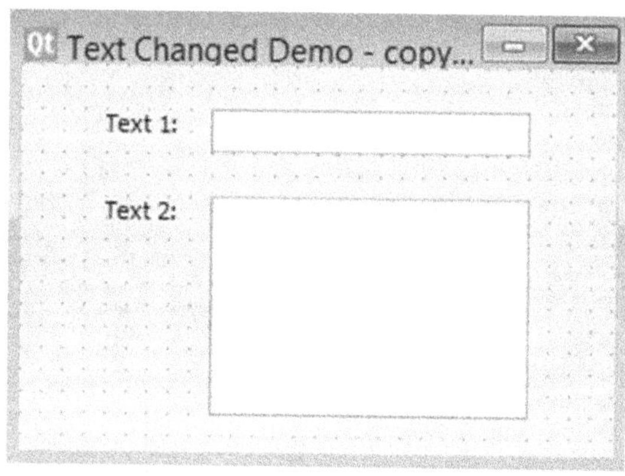

Here is how the PyQt/Python equivalent script (***copytextonthefly_ui***) looks like after running the ***pyuic5*** command:

```
# -*- coding: utf-8 -*-
# Form implementation generated from reading ui file
'copytextonthefly.ui'
# Created by: PyQt5 UI code generator 5.13.0
# WARNING! All changes made in this file will be lost!

from PyQt5 import QtCore, QtGui, QtWidgets

class Ui_Dialog(object):
    def setupUi(self, Dialog):
        Dialog.setObjectName("Dialog")
        Dialog.resize(282, 178)
        self.label = QtWidgets.QLabel(Dialog)
        self.label.setGeometry(QtCore.QRect(40, 20,
        47, 13))
        self.label.setObjectName("label")
        self.label_2 = QtWidgets.QLabel(Dialog)
```

```
        self.label_2.setGeometry(QtCore.QRect(40, 60,
        47, 13))
        self.label_2.setObjectName("label_2")
        self.lineEdit_src =
        QtWidgets.QLineEdit(Dialog)
        self.lineEdit_src.setGeometry(QtCore.QRect(90,
        20, 151, 20))
        self.lineEdit_src.setObjectName("lineEdit_src")
        self.plainTextEdit_dest =
        QtWidgets.QPlainTextEdit(Dialog)
        self.plainTextEdit_dest.setGeometry(QtCore.QRe
        ct(90, 60, 151, 101))
        self.plainTextEdit_dest.setObjectName("plainTe
        xtEdit_dest")

        self.retranslateUi(Dialog)
        QtCore.QMetaObject.connectSlotsByName(Dialog)

    def retranslateUi(self, Dialog):
        _translate = QtCore.QCoreApplication.translate
        Dialog.setWindowTitle(_translate("Dialog",
        "Text Changed Demo"))
        self.label.setText(_translate("Dialog", "Text
        1:"))
        self.label_2.setText(_translate("Dialog",
        "Text 2:"))
```

Here is how the main script derived from PyQt5 App Skeleton Code to launch our UI looks like ***(start_copytextonthefly.py)***:

```
import sys
from PyQt5.QtWidgets import QDialog, QApplication
from copytextonthefly_ui import Ui_Dialog

#Create a class for the application window
class CopyTextOTFDialog(QDialog):
    #Slot to handle lineEdit_src's text changed event
    def lineEdit_src_textChanged(self):
        #Fetch text from the line edit
        text = self.ui.lineEdit_src.text()
        #Print on the terminal
        print ("Text Changed!: ", text)
        #Copy to the plainTextEdit
        self.ui.plainTextEdit_dest.setPlainText(text)
    #Constructor function
    def __init__(self):
```

```
        #Call super-class constructor
        super().__init__()
        #Initialize and setup UI
        self.ui = Ui_Dialog()
        self.ui.setupUi(self)
        #Connect lineEdit_src's textChanged signal to
        lineEdit_src_textChanged
    self.ui.lineEdit_src.textChanged.connect(self.line
    Edit_src_textChanged)
        #Make UI Visible
        self.show()
#Main routine
if (__name__ == "__main__"):
    #Create an application instance of QApplication
    type
    app = QApplication(sys.argv)
    #Create an app window
    appwindow = CopyTextOTFDialog()
    #Show the app window using show() function
    appwindow.show()
    #Keep the script active until the app closes
    sys.exit(app.exec_())
```

The ***textChanged*** event of ***lineEdit_src*** has been connected to the slot function ***lineEdit_src_textChanged*** which prints on the terminal every time the user changes the text and copies to ***plainTextEdit_dest*** at the same time. Run this script, wait for the UI to launch and enter something in the line edit. This is what you will see:

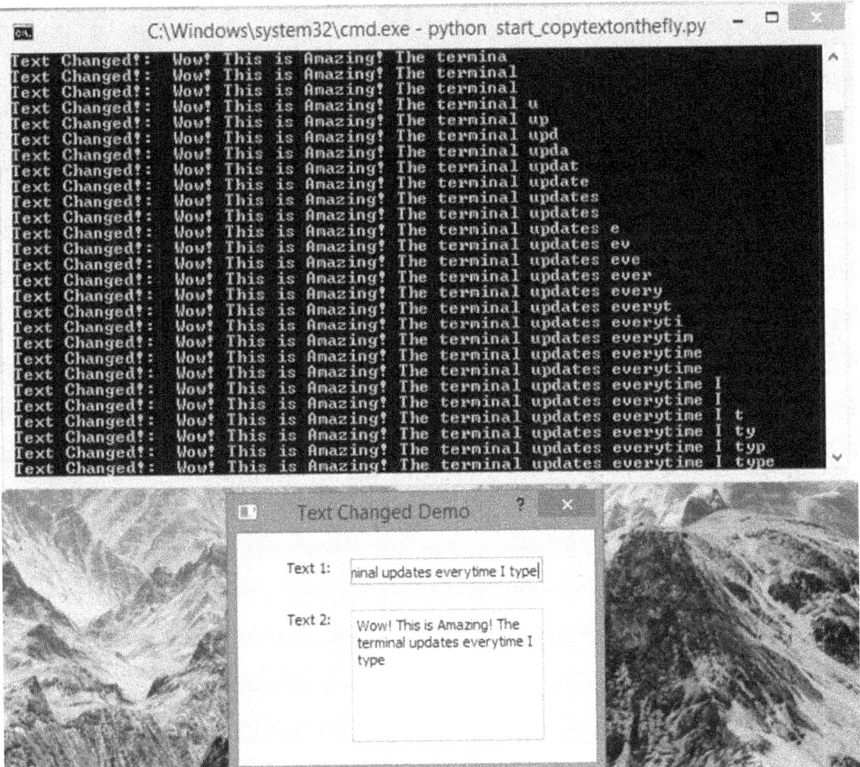

20.3 Combo Box Selection Changed

Whenever a user selects an item from a combo box, this event emits a signal called ***"currentTextChanged"***. If you had a combo box called ***comboBox_question*** and wanted to call a slot function ***item_changed***, you would connect the signal to this slot in the following way:

self.ui.comboBox_question.currentTextChanged.connect(self.item_changed)

Let us build a PyQt App with one Combo Box. We will populate this combo box with the names of a few countries. Every time the user selects a different item, the text of the newly selected item should be printed in the terminal. This is how our simplistic UI will look like:

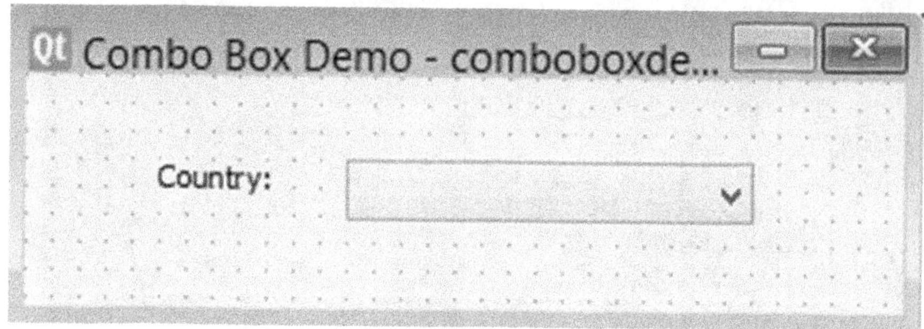

Once this QML UI file is converted to PyQt script, this is what it looks like *(comboboxdemo_ui.py)*:

```
# -*- coding: utf-8 -*-
# Form implementation generated from reading ui file
'comboboxdemo.ui'
# Created by: PyQt5 UI code generator 5.13.0
# WARNING! All changes made in this file will be lost!

from PyQt5 import QtCore, QtGui, QtWidgets

class Ui_Dialog(object):
    def setupUi(self, Dialog):
        Dialog.setObjectName("Dialog")
        Dialog.resize(327, 84)
        self.label = QtWidgets.QLabel(Dialog)
        self.label.setGeometry(QtCore.QRect(50, 30,
        47, 13))
        self.label.setObjectName("label")
        self.comboBox_country =
        QtWidgets.QComboBox(Dialog)
        self.comboBox_country.setGeometry(QtCore.QRect
        (120, 30, 151, 22))
        self.comboBox_country.setObjectName("comboBox_
        country")

        self.retranslateUi(Dialog)
        QtCore.QMetaObject.connectSlotsByName(Dialog)

    def retranslateUi(self, Dialog):
        _translate = QtCore.QCoreApplication.translate
```

```
Dialog.setWindowTitle(_translate("Dialog",
"Combo Box Demo"))
self.label.setText(_translate("Dialog",
"Country:"))
```

The main script derived from PyQt5 App Skeleton Code to launch our UI looks like this ***(start_comboboxdemo.py)***:

```
import sys
from PyQt5.QtWidgets import QDialog, QApplication
from comboboxdemo_ui import Ui_Dialog

#Create a class for the application window
class ComboBoxDemoDialog(QDialog):
    #Slot to handle comboBox_country's
    currentTextChanged event
    def comboBox_country_item_changed(self):
        #Fetch text from the comboBox
        country =
        self.ui.comboBox_country.currentText()
        #Print on the terminal
        print ("Country Changed - ", country)

    #Constructor function
    def __init__(self):
        #Call super-class constructor
        super().__init__()
        #Initialize and setup UI
        self.ui = Ui_Dialog()
        self.ui.setupUi(self)
        #Add some countries' names to comboBox_country
        self.ui.comboBox_country.addItem("Australia")
        self.ui.comboBox_country.addItem("Belgium")
        self.ui.comboBox_country.addItem("Canada")
        self.ui.comboBox_country.addItem("Denmark")
        self.ui.comboBox_country.addItem("Estonia")
        self.ui.comboBox_country.addItem("Finland")
        self.ui.comboBox_country.addItem("Germany")
        self.ui.comboBox_country.addItem("Hungary")
        self.ui.comboBox_country.addItem("Iceland")
        self.ui.comboBox_country.addItem("Japan")
        #Connect comboBox_country's currentTextChanged
        signal to comboBox_country_item_changed
    self.ui.comboBox_country.currentTextChanged.connec
    t(self.comboBox_country_item_changed)
        #Make UI Visible
```

```
        self.show()
#Main routine
if (__name__ == "__main__"):
    #Create an application instance of QApplication
    type
    app = QApplication(sys.argv)
    #Create an app window
    appwindow = ComboBoxDemoDialog()
    #Show the app window using show() function
    appwindow.show()
    #Keep the script active until the app closes
    sys.exit(app.exec_())
```

This is what you will see when you run the script and change country:

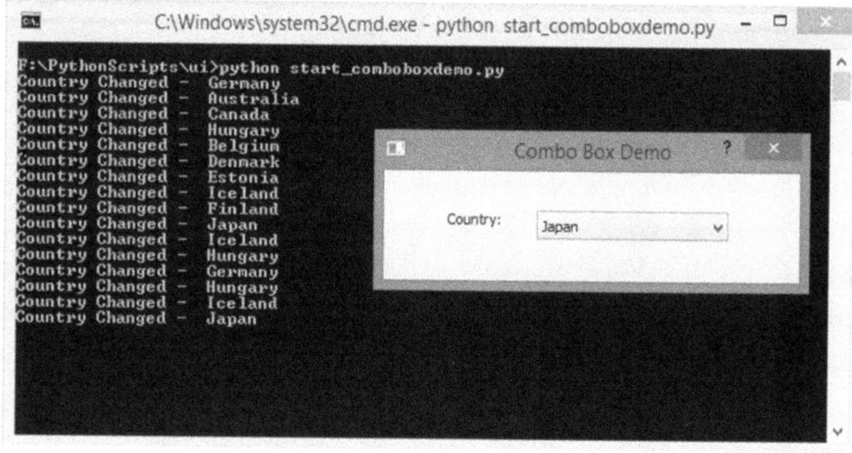

21. Final Words

Python is an incredibly useful programming langue. You can do almost everything with it. Being a cross platform, general purpose object oriented scripting language, Python is used in desktop applications, web applications/services, embedded systems, Internet of Things (IoT), data science, machine learning, etc.

Whenever you learn a new programming language, especially if you are new to programming, you have to make sure that you understand the basic concepts very well. Hence, in this book I have tried my level best to break down concepts and explain them in the simplest possible manner. If you follow this book chapter by chapter, you should be able to write basic Python scripts and be able to build simple GUI apps using PyQt.

If you have developed a liking for Python, I strongly suggest learning more advanced topics such as File I/O, exception handling, object oriented programming, socket programming, etc. You could also dive deeper into PyQt. There are many frameworks/libraries in Python used for different things. For example, TensorFlow is used for Machine Learning, PySpark (Python binding for Apache Spark) is used for Data Science, Django and Flask are used for building REST APIs, and many more… Based on your area of interest, you could learn these frameworks once you have a good command over Python. There are myriad resources online.

Hope you have learned something of value from my Book!

Good Luck!

If you enjoyed this book as much as I've enjoyed writing it, you can subscribe* to my email list for exclusive content and sneak peaks of my future books.

Visit the link below:

http://eepurl.com/du_L4n

OR

Use the QR Code:

(*Must be 13 years or older to subscribe)

www.ingramcontent.com/pod-product-compliance
Lightning Source LLC
Chambersburg PA
CBHW031241050326
40690CB00007B/902

* 9 7 8 1 6 5 0 4 4 0 7 1 2 *